ADHI
Planner

INFORMATION

NAME

ADDRESS

E-MAIL ADDRESS

WEBSITE

PHONE   **FAX**

EMERGENCY CONTACTS

DAY GOALS

1. ADHD what is.
2. Bad ADHD GPH
3. ....

DATE 15/10/21

WEEK 1

LOCATION Home

WEIGHT

MOOD TRACKER

$\odot$ $\odot$ $\odot$ $\odot$ $\odot$ $\odot$

BEHAVIOR

INATTENTION

SHORT ATTENTION	① ② ③ ④ ⑤ ⑥ ⑦ ⑧ ⑨ ⑩
UNMOTIVATED / BORED	① ② ③ ④ ⑤ ⑥ ⑦ ⑧ ⑨ ⑩
SHORT ATTENTION	① ② ③ ④ ⑤ ⑥ ⑦ ⑧ ⑨ ⑩
FORGETFUL / CONFUSIONED	① ② ③ ④ ⑤ ⑥ ⑦ ⑧ ⑨ ⑩

HYPERACTIVITY

CONSTANTLY MOVING / TALKING	① ② ③ ④ ⑤ ⑥ ⑦ ⑧ ⑨ ⑩
STRUGGLING TO SIT STILL	① ② ③ ④ ⑤ ⑥ ⑦ ⑧ ⑨ ⑩
TOUCHING THINGS REPEATEDLY	① ② ③ ④ ⑤ ⑥ ⑦ ⑧ ⑨ ⑩
DIFFICULT SLEEPING	① ② ③ ④ ⑤ ⑥ ⑦ ⑧ ⑨ ⑩

IMPULSIVITY

ACTING WITHOUT THINKING	① ② ③ ④ ⑤ ⑥ ⑦ ⑧ ⑨ ⑩
INTERRUPTING OTHERS	① ② ③ ④ ⑤ ⑥ ⑦ ⑧ ⑨ ⑩
EASILY FRUSTRATED	① ② ③ ④ ⑤ ⑥ ⑦ ⑧ ⑨ ⑩
UNABLE TO HOLD BACKE MOTIONS	① ② ③ ④ ⑤ ⑥ ⑦ ⑧ ⑨ ⑩

MEALS

MEDICATIONS

WATER TRACKER

NOTES

MOOD TRACKER

BEHAVIOR

INATTENTION

SHORT ATTENTION	①②③④⑤⑥⑦⑧⑨⑩
UNMOTIVATED / BORED	①②③④⑤⑥⑦⑧⑨⑩
SHORT ATTENTION	①②③④⑤⑥⑦⑧⑨⑩
FORGETFUL / CONFUSIONED	①②③④⑤⑥⑦⑧⑨⑩

HYPERACTIVITY

CONSTANTLY MOVING / TALKING	①②③④⑤⑥⑦⑧⑨⑩
STRUGGLING TO SIT STILL	①②③④⑤⑥⑦⑧⑨⑩
TOUCHING THINGS REPEATEDLY	①②③④⑤⑥⑦⑧⑨⑩
DIFFICULT SLEEPING	①②③④⑤⑥⑦⑧⑨⑩

IMPULSIVITY

ACTING WITHOUT THINKING	①②③④⑤⑥⑦⑧⑨⑩
INTERRUPTING OTHERS	①②③④⑤⑥⑦⑧⑨⑩
EASILY FRUSTRATED	①②③④⑤⑥⑦⑧⑨⑩
UNABLE TO HOLD BACKE MOTIONS	①②③④⑤⑥⑦⑧⑨⑩

MEALS

MEDICATIONS

WATER TRACKER

NOTES

....
....

MOOD TRACKER

BEHAVIOR

INATTENTION

SHORT ATTENTION	① ② ③ ④ ⑤ ⑥ ⑦ ⑧ ⑨ ⑩
UNMOTIVATED / BORED	① ② ③ ④ ⑤ ⑥ ⑦ ⑧ ⑨ ⑩
SHORT ATTENTION	① ② ③ ④ ⑤ ⑥ ⑦ ⑧ ⑨ ⑩
FORGETFUL / CONFUSIONED	① ② ③ ④ ⑤ ⑥ ⑦ ⑧ ⑨ ⑩

HYPERACTIVITY

CONSTANTLY MOVING / TALKING	① ② ③ ④ ⑤ ⑥ ⑦ ⑧ ⑨ ⑩
STRUGGLING TO SIT STILL	① ② ③ ④ ⑤ ⑥ ⑦ ⑧ ⑨ ⑩
TOUCHING THINGS REPEATEDLY	① ② ③ ④ ⑤ ⑥ ⑦ ⑧ ⑨ ⑩
DIFFICULT SLEEPING	① ② ③ ④ ⑤ ⑥ ⑦ ⑧ ⑨ ⑩

IMPULSIVITY

ACTING WITHOUT THINKING	① ② ③ ④ ⑤ ⑥ ⑦ ⑧ ⑨ ⑩
INTERRUPTING OTHERS	① ② ③ ④ ⑤ ⑥ ⑦ ⑧ ⑨ ⑩
EASILY FRUSTRATED	① ② ③ ④ ⑤ ⑥ ⑦ ⑧ ⑨ ⑩
UNABLE TO HOLD BACKE MOTIONS	① ② ③ ④ ⑤ ⑥ ⑦ ⑧ ⑨ ⑩

MEALS	MEDICATIONS

WATER TRACKER

NOTES

....
....

DAY GOALS

1 ....
2 ....
3 ....

DATE

WEEK

LOCATION

WEIGHT

MOOD TRACKER

BEHAVIOR

INATTENTION

SHORT ATTENTION	① ② ③ ④ ⑤ ⑥ ⑦ ⑧ ⑨ ⑩
UNMOTIVATED / BORED	① ② ③ ④ ⑤ ⑥ ⑦ ⑧ ⑨ ⑩
SHORT ATTENTION	① ② ③ ④ ⑤ ⑥ ⑦ ⑧ ⑨ ⑩
FORGETFUL / CONFUSIONED	① ② ③ ④ ⑤ ⑥ ⑦ ⑧ ⑨ ⑩

HYPERACTIVITY

CONSTANTLY MOVING / TALKING	① ② ③ ④ ⑤ ⑥ ⑦ ⑧ ⑨ ⑩
STRUGGLING TO SIT STILL	① ② ③ ④ ⑤ ⑥ ⑦ ⑧ ⑨ ⑩
TOUCHING THINGS REPEATEDLY	① ② ③ ④ ⑤ ⑥ ⑦ ⑧ ⑨ ⑩
DIFFICULT SLEEPING	① ② ③ ④ ⑤ ⑥ ⑦ ⑧ ⑨ ⑩

IMPULSIVITY

ACTING WITHOUT THINKING	① ② ③ ④ ⑤ ⑥ ⑦ ⑧ ⑨ ⑩
INTERRUPTING OTHERS	① ② ③ ④ ⑤ ⑥ ⑦ ⑧ ⑨ ⑩
EASILY FRUSTRATED	① ② ③ ④ ⑤ ⑥ ⑦ ⑧ ⑨ ⑩
UNABLE TO HOLD BACKE MOTIONS	① ② ③ ④ ⑤ ⑥ ⑦ ⑧ ⑨ ⑩

MEALS

MEDICATIONS

WATER TRACKER

NOTES

....
....

DAY GOALS

1 ....
2 ....
3 ....

DATE

WEEK

LOCATION

WEIGHT

MOOD TRACKER

BEHAVIOR

INATTENTION

SHORT ATTENTION	① ② ③ ④ ⑤ ⑥ ⑦ ⑧ ⑨ ⑩
UNMOTIVATED / BORED	① ② ③ ④ ⑤ ⑥ ⑦ ⑧ ⑨ ⑩
SHORT ATTENTION	① ② ③ ④ ⑤ ⑥ ⑦ ⑧ ⑨ ⑩
FORGETFUL / CONFUSIONED	① ② ③ ④ ⑤ ⑥ ⑦ ⑧ ⑨ ⑩

HYPERACTIVITY

CONSTANTLY MOVING / TALKING	① ② ③ ④ ⑤ ⑥ ⑦ ⑧ ⑨ ⑩
STRUGGLING TO SIT STILL	① ② ③ ④ ⑤ ⑥ ⑦ ⑧ ⑨ ⑩
TOUCHING THINGS REPEATEDLY	① ② ③ ④ ⑤ ⑥ ⑦ ⑧ ⑨ ⑩
DIFFICULT SLEEPING	① ② ③ ④ ⑤ ⑥ ⑦ ⑧ ⑨ ⑩

IMPULSIVITY

ACTING WITHOUT THINKING	① ② ③ ④ ⑤ ⑥ ⑦ ⑧ ⑨ ⑩
INTERRUPTING OTHERS	① ② ③ ④ ⑤ ⑥ ⑦ ⑧ ⑨ ⑩
EASILY FRUSTRATED	① ② ③ ④ ⑤ ⑥ ⑦ ⑧ ⑨ ⑩
UNABLE TO HOLD BACKE MOTIONS	① ② ③ ④ ⑤ ⑥ ⑦ ⑧ ⑨ ⑩

MEALS

MEDICATIONS

WATER TRACKER

NOTES

....
....

DAY GOALS

1 ....
2 ....
3 ....

DATE

WEEK

LOCATION

WEIGHT

MOOD TRACKER

BEHAVIOR

INATTENTION

SHORT ATTENTION	① ② ③ ④ ⑤ ⑥ ⑦ ⑧ ⑨ ⑩
UNMOTIVATED / BORED	① ② ③ ④ ⑤ ⑥ ⑦ ⑧ ⑨ ⑩
SHORT ATTENTION	① ② ③ ④ ⑤ ⑥ ⑦ ⑧ ⑨ ⑩
FORGETFUL / CONFUSIONED	① ② ③ ④ ⑤ ⑥ ⑦ ⑧ ⑨ ⑩

HYPERACTIVITY

CONSTANTLY MOVING / TALKING	① ② ③ ④ ⑤ ⑥ ⑦ ⑧ ⑨ ⑩
STRUGGLING TO SIT STILL	① ② ③ ④ ⑤ ⑥ ⑦ ⑧ ⑨ ⑩
TOUCHING THINGS REPEATEDLY	① ② ③ ④ ⑤ ⑥ ⑦ ⑧ ⑨ ⑩
DIFFICULT SLEEPING	① ② ③ ④ ⑤ ⑥ ⑦ ⑧ ⑨ ⑩

IMPULSIVITY

ACTING WITHOUT THINKING	① ② ③ ④ ⑤ ⑥ ⑦ ⑧ ⑨ ⑩
INTERRUPTING OTHERS	① ② ③ ④ ⑤ ⑥ ⑦ ⑧ ⑨ ⑩
EASILY FRUSTRATED	① ② ③ ④ ⑤ ⑥ ⑦ ⑧ ⑨ ⑩
UNABLE TO HOLD BACKE MOTIONS	① ② ③ ④ ⑤ ⑥ ⑦ ⑧ ⑨ ⑩

MEALS

MEDICATIONS

WATER TRACKER

NOTES

....
....

DAY GOALS

1 ....
2 ....
3 ....

DATE

WEEK

LOCATION

WEIGHT

MOOD TRACKER

😕 😐 😣 😢 😠 😃

BEHAVIOR

INATTENTION

SHORT ATTENTION	① ② ③ ④ ⑤ ⑥ ⑦ ⑧ ⑨ ⑩
UNMOTIVATED / BORED	① ② ③ ④ ⑤ ⑥ ⑦ ⑧ ⑨ ⑩
SHORT ATTENTION	① ② ③ ④ ⑤ ⑥ ⑦ ⑧ ⑨ ⑩
FORGETFUL / CONFUSIONED	① ② ③ ④ ⑤ ⑥ ⑦ ⑧ ⑨ ⑩

HYPERACTIVITY

CONSTANTLY MOVING / TALKING	① ② ③ ④ ⑤ ⑥ ⑦ ⑧ ⑨ ⑩
STRUGGLING TO SIT STILL	① ② ③ ④ ⑤ ⑥ ⑦ ⑧ ⑨ ⑩
TOUCHING THINGS REPEATEDLY	① ② ③ ④ ⑤ ⑥ ⑦ ⑧ ⑨ ⑩
DIFFICULT SLEEPING	① ② ③ ④ ⑤ ⑥ ⑦ ⑧ ⑨ ⑩

IMPULSIVITY

ACTING WITHOUT THINKING	① ② ③ ④ ⑤ ⑥ ⑦ ⑧ ⑨ ⑩
INTERRUPTING OTHERS	① ② ③ ④ ⑤ ⑥ ⑦ ⑧ ⑨ ⑩
EASILY FRUSTRATED	① ② ③ ④ ⑤ ⑥ ⑦ ⑧ ⑨ ⑩
UNABLE TO HOLD BACKE MOTIONS	① ② ③ ④ ⑤ ⑥ ⑦ ⑧ ⑨ ⑩

MEALS

MEDICATIONS

WATER TRACKER

⬜ ⬜ ⬜ ⬜ ⬜ ⬜ ⬜

NOTES

....
....

DAY GOALS

1 ....
2 ....
3 ....

DATE

WEEK

LOCATION

WEIGHT

MOOD TRACKER

BEHAVIOR

INATTENTION

SHORT ATTENTION	① ② ③ ④ ⑤ ⑥ ⑦ ⑧ ⑨ ⑩
UNMOTIVATED / BORED	① ② ③ ④ ⑤ ⑥ ⑦ ⑧ ⑨ ⑩
SHORT ATTENTION	① ② ③ ④ ⑤ ⑥ ⑦ ⑧ ⑨ ⑩
FORGETFUL / CONFUSIONED	① ② ③ ④ ⑤ ⑥ ⑦ ⑧ ⑨ ⑩

HYPERACTIVITY

CONSTANTLY MOVING / TALKING	① ② ③ ④ ⑤ ⑥ ⑦ ⑧ ⑨ ⑩
STRUGGLING TO SIT STILL	① ② ③ ④ ⑤ ⑥ ⑦ ⑧ ⑨ ⑩
TOUCHING THINGS REPEATEDLY	① ② ③ ④ ⑤ ⑥ ⑦ ⑧ ⑨ ⑩
DIFFICULT SLEEPING	① ② ③ ④ ⑤ ⑥ ⑦ ⑧ ⑨ ⑩

IMPULSIVITY

ACTING WITHOUT THINKING	① ② ③ ④ ⑤ ⑥ ⑦ ⑧ ⑨ ⑩
INTERRUPTING OTHERS	① ② ③ ④ ⑤ ⑥ ⑦ ⑧ ⑨ ⑩
EASILY FRUSTRATED	① ② ③ ④ ⑤ ⑥ ⑦ ⑧ ⑨ ⑩
UNABLE TO HOLD BACKE MOTIONS	① ② ③ ④ ⑤ ⑥ ⑦ ⑧ ⑨ ⑩

MEALS

MEDICATIONS

WATER TRACKER

NOTES

....
....

MOOD TRACKER

BEHAVIOR

INATTENTION

SHORT ATTENTION	1 2 3 4 5 6 7 8 9 10
UNMOTIVATED / BORED	1 2 3 4 5 6 7 8 9 10
SHORT ATTENTION	1 2 3 4 5 6 7 8 9 10
FORGETFUL / CONFUSIONED	1 2 3 4 5 6 7 8 9 10

HYPERACTIVITY

CONSTANTLY MOVING / TALKING	1 2 3 4 5 6 7 8 9 10
STRUGGLING TO SIT STILL	1 2 3 4 5 6 7 8 9 10
TOUCHING THINGS REPEATEDLY	1 2 3 4 5 6 7 8 9 10
DIFFICULT SLEEPING	1 2 3 4 5 6 7 8 9 10

IMPULSIVITY

ACTING WITHOUT THINKING	1 2 3 4 5 6 7 8 9 10
INTERRUPTING OTHERS	1 2 3 4 5 6 7 8 9 10
EASILY FRUSTRATED	1 2 3 4 5 6 7 8 9 10
UNABLE TO HOLD BACKE MOTIONS	1 2 3 4 5 6 7 8 9 10

MEALS

MEDICATIONS

WATER TRACKER

NOTES

....
....

DAY GOALS

1 ....
2 ....
3 ....

DATE

WEEK

LOCATION

WEIGHT

MOOD TRACKER

BEHAVIOR

INATTENTION

SHORT ATTENTION	① ② ③ ④ ⑤ ⑥ ⑦ ⑧ ⑨ ⑩
SHORT ATTENTION	① ② ③ ④ ⑤ ⑥ ⑦ ⑧ ⑨ ⑩
UNMOTIVATED / BORED	① ② ③ ④ ⑤ ⑥ ⑦ ⑧ ⑨ ⑩
SHORT ATTENTION	① ② ③ ④ ⑤ ⑥ ⑦ ⑧ ⑨ ⑩
FORGETFUL / CONFUSIONED	① ② ③ ④ ⑤ ⑥ ⑦ ⑧ ⑨ ⑩

HYPERACTIVITY

CONSTANTLY MOVING / TALKING	① ② ③ ④ ⑤ ⑥ ⑦ ⑧ ⑨ ⑩
STRUGGLING TO SIT STILL	① ② ③ ④ ⑤ ⑥ ⑦ ⑧ ⑨ ⑩
TOUCHING THINGS REPEATEDLY	① ② ③ ④ ⑤ ⑥ ⑦ ⑧ ⑨ ⑩
DIFFICULT SLEEPING	① ② ③ ④ ⑤ ⑥ ⑦ ⑧ ⑨ ⑩

IMPULSIVITY

ACTING WITHOUT THINKING	① ② ③ ④ ⑤ ⑥ ⑦ ⑧ ⑨ ⑩
INTERRUPTING OTHERS	① ② ③ ④ ⑤ ⑥ ⑦ ⑧ ⑨ ⑩
EASILY FRUSTRATED	① ② ③ ④ ⑤ ⑥ ⑦ ⑧ ⑨ ⑩
UNABLE TO HOLD BACKE MOTIONS	① ② ③ ④ ⑤ ⑥ ⑦ ⑧ ⑨ ⑩

MEALS

MEDICATIONS

WATER TRACKER

NOTES

....
....

DAY GOALS

1 ....
2 ....
3 ....

DATE

WEEK

LOCATION

WEIGHT

MOOD TRACKER

BEHAVIOR

INATTENTION

SHORT ATTENTION	① ② ③ ④ ⑤ ⑥ ⑦ ⑧ ⑨ ⑩
UNMOTIVATED / BORED	① ② ③ ④ ⑤ ⑥ ⑦ ⑧ ⑨ ⑩
SHORT ATTENTION	① ② ③ ④ ⑤ ⑥ ⑦ ⑧ ⑨ ⑩
FORGETFUL / CONFUSIONED	① ② ③ ④ ⑤ ⑥ ⑦ ⑧ ⑨ ⑩

HYPERACTIVITY

CONSTANTLY MOVING / TALKING	① ② ③ ④ ⑤ ⑥ ⑦ ⑧ ⑨ ⑩
STRUGGLING TO SIT STILL	① ② ③ ④ ⑤ ⑥ ⑦ ⑧ ⑨ ⑩
TOUCHING THINGS REPEATEDLY	① ② ③ ④ ⑤ ⑥ ⑦ ⑧ ⑨ ⑩
DIFFICULT SLEEPING	① ② ③ ④ ⑤ ⑥ ⑦ ⑧ ⑨ ⑩

IMPULSIVITY

ACTING WITHOUT THINKING	① ② ③ ④ ⑤ ⑥ ⑦ ⑧ ⑨ ⑩
INTERRUPTING OTHERS	① ② ③ ④ ⑤ ⑥ ⑦ ⑧ ⑨ ⑩
EASILY FRUSTRATED	① ② ③ ④ ⑤ ⑥ ⑦ ⑧ ⑨ ⑩
UNABLE TO HOLD BACKE MOTIONS	① ② ③ ④ ⑤ ⑥ ⑦ ⑧ ⑨ ⑩

MEALS

MEDICATIONS

WATER TRACKER

NOTES

....
....

MOOD TRACKER 😕 😐 >< 😢 😠 😄

BEHAVIOR

INATTENTION

SHORT ATTENTION	① ② ③ ④ ⑤ ⑥ ⑦ ⑧ ⑨ ⑩
UNMOTIVATED / BORED	① ② ③ ④ ⑤ ⑥ ⑦ ⑧ ⑨ ⑩
SHORT ATTENTION	① ② ③ ④ ⑤ ⑥ ⑦ ⑧ ⑨ ⑩
FORGETFUL / CONFUSIONED	① ② ③ ④ ⑤ ⑥ ⑦ ⑧ ⑨ ⑩

HYPERACTIVITY

CONSTANTLY MOVING / TALKING	① ② ③ ④ ⑤ ⑥ ⑦ ⑧ ⑨ ⑩
STRUGGLING TO SIT STILL	① ② ③ ④ ⑤ ⑥ ⑦ ⑧ ⑨ ⑩
TOUCHING THINGS REPEATEDLY	① ② ③ ④ ⑤ ⑥ ⑦ ⑧ ⑨ ⑩
DIFFICULT SLEEPING	① ② ③ ④ ⑤ ⑥ ⑦ ⑧ ⑨ ⑩

IMPULSIVITY

ACTING WITHOUT THINKING	① ② ③ ④ ⑤ ⑥ ⑦ ⑧ ⑨ ⑩
INTERRUPTING OTHERS	① ② ③ ④ ⑤ ⑥ ⑦ ⑧ ⑨ ⑩
EASILY FRUSTRATED	① ② ③ ④ ⑤ ⑥ ⑦ ⑧ ⑨ ⑩
UNABLE TO HOLD BACKE MOTIONS	① ② ③ ④ ⑤ ⑥ ⑦ ⑧ ⑨ ⑩

MEALS	MEDICATIONS

WATER TRACKER ▭ ▭ ▭ ▭ ▭ ▭ ▭

NOTES

....
....

MOOD TRACKER :-(:-| >< ~~ :-(>:v :-D

BEHAVIOR

INATTENTION

SHORT ATTENTION	① ② ③ ④ ⑤ ⑥ ⑦ ⑧ ⑨ ⑩
UNMOTIVATED / BORED	① ② ③ ④ ⑤ ⑥ ⑦ ⑧ ⑨ ⑩
SHORT ATTENTION	① ② ③ ④ ⑤ ⑥ ⑦ ⑧ ⑨ ⑩
FORGETFUL / CONFUSIONED	① ② ③ ④ ⑤ ⑥ ⑦ ⑧ ⑨ ⑩

HYPERACTIVITY

CONSTANTLY MOVING / TALKING	① ② ③ ④ ⑤ ⑥ ⑦ ⑧ ⑨ ⑩
STRUGGLING TO SIT STILL	① ② ③ ④ ⑤ ⑥ ⑦ ⑧ ⑨ ⑩
TOUCHING THINGS REPEATEDLY	① ② ③ ④ ⑤ ⑥ ⑦ ⑧ ⑨ ⑩
DIFFICULT SLEEPING	① ② ③ ④ ⑤ ⑥ ⑦ ⑧ ⑨ ⑩

IMPULSIVITY

ACTING WITHOUT THINKING	① ② ③ ④ ⑤ ⑥ ⑦ ⑧ ⑨ ⑩
INTERRUPTING OTHERS	① ② ③ ④ ⑤ ⑥ ⑦ ⑧ ⑨ ⑩
EASILY FRUSTRATED	① ② ③ ④ ⑤ ⑥ ⑦ ⑧ ⑨ ⑩
UNABLE TO HOLD BACKE MOTIONS	① ② ③ ④ ⑤ ⑥ ⑦ ⑧ ⑨ ⑩

MEALS	MEDICATIONS

WATER TRACKER ☐ ☐ ☐ ☐ ☐ ☐ ☐

NOTES

....
....

DAY GOALS

1 ....
2 ....
3 ....

DATE

WEEK

LOCATION

WEIGHT

MOOD TRACKER

BEHAVIOR

INATTENTION

SHORT ATTENTION	① ② ③ ④ ⑤ ⑥ ⑦ ⑧ ⑨ ⑩
UNMOTIVATED / BORED	① ② ③ ④ ⑤ ⑥ ⑦ ⑧ ⑨ ⑩
SHORT ATTENTION	① ② ③ ④ ⑤ ⑥ ⑦ ⑧ ⑨ ⑩
FORGETFUL / CONFUSIONED	① ② ③ ④ ⑤ ⑥ ⑦ ⑧ ⑨ ⑩

HYPERACTIVITY

CONSTANTLY MOVING / TALKING	① ② ③ ④ ⑤ ⑥ ⑦ ⑧ ⑨ ⑩
STRUGGLING TO SIT STILL	① ② ③ ④ ⑤ ⑥ ⑦ ⑧ ⑨ ⑩
TOUCHING THINGS REPEATEDLY	① ② ③ ④ ⑤ ⑥ ⑦ ⑧ ⑨ ⑩
DIFFICULT SLEEPING	① ② ③ ④ ⑤ ⑥ ⑦ ⑧ ⑨ ⑩

IMPULSIVITY

ACTING WITHOUT THINKING	① ② ③ ④ ⑤ ⑥ ⑦ ⑧ ⑨ ⑩
INTERRUPTING OTHERS	① ② ③ ④ ⑤ ⑥ ⑦ ⑧ ⑨ ⑩
EASILY FRUSTRATED	① ② ③ ④ ⑤ ⑥ ⑦ ⑧ ⑨ ⑩
UNABLE TO HOLD BACKE MOTIONS	① ② ③ ④ ⑤ ⑥ ⑦ ⑧ ⑨ ⑩

MEALS

MEDICATIONS

WATER TRACKER

NOTES

....
....

MOOD TRACKER

BEHAVIOR

INATTENTION

SHORT ATTENTION	① ② ③ ④ ⑤ ⑥ ⑦ ⑧ ⑨ ⑩
UNMOTIVATED / BORED	① ② ③ ④ ⑤ ⑥ ⑦ ⑧ ⑨ ⑩
SHORT ATTENTION	① ② ③ ④ ⑤ ⑥ ⑦ ⑧ ⑨ ⑩
FORGETFUL / CONFUSIONED	① ② ③ ④ ⑤ ⑥ ⑦ ⑧ ⑨ ⑩

HYPERACTIVITY

CONSTANTLY MOVING / TALKING	① ② ③ ④ ⑤ ⑥ ⑦ ⑧ ⑨ ⑩
STRUGGLING TO SIT STILL	① ② ③ ④ ⑤ ⑥ ⑦ ⑧ ⑨ ⑩
TOUCHING THINGS REPEATEDLY	① ② ③ ④ ⑤ ⑥ ⑦ ⑧ ⑨ ⑩
DIFFICULT SLEEPING	① ② ③ ④ ⑤ ⑥ ⑦ ⑧ ⑨ ⑩

IMPULSIVITY

ACTING WITHOUT THINKING	① ② ③ ④ ⑤ ⑥ ⑦ ⑧ ⑨ ⑩
INTERRUPTING OTHERS	① ② ③ ④ ⑤ ⑥ ⑦ ⑧ ⑨ ⑩
EASILY FRUSTRATED	① ② ③ ④ ⑤ ⑥ ⑦ ⑧ ⑨ ⑩
UNABLE TO HOLD BACKE MOTIONS	① ② ③ ④ ⑤ ⑥ ⑦ ⑧ ⑨ ⑩

MEALS	MEDICATIONS

WATER TRACKER

NOTES

....
....

DAY GOALS

1 ....
2 ....
3 ....

DATE

WEEK

LOCATION

WEIGHT

MOOD TRACKER

BEHAVIOR

INATTENTION

SHORT ATTENTION	① ② ③ ④ ⑤ ⑥ ⑦ ⑧ ⑨ ⑩
UNMOTIVATED / BORED	① ② ③ ④ ⑤ ⑥ ⑦ ⑧ ⑨ ⑩
SHORT ATTENTION	① ② ③ ④ ⑤ ⑥ ⑦ ⑧ ⑨ ⑩
FORGETFUL / CONFUSIONED	① ② ③ ④ ⑤ ⑥ ⑦ ⑧ ⑨ ⑩

HYPERACTIVITY

CONSTANTLY MOVING / TALKING	① ② ③ ④ ⑤ ⑥ ⑦ ⑧ ⑨ ⑩
STRUGGLING TO SIT STILL	① ② ③ ④ ⑤ ⑥ ⑦ ⑧ ⑨ ⑩
TOUCHING THINGS REPEATEDLY	① ② ③ ④ ⑤ ⑥ ⑦ ⑧ ⑨ ⑩
DIFFICULT SLEEPING	① ② ③ ④ ⑤ ⑥ ⑦ ⑧ ⑨ ⑩

IMPULSIVITY

ACTING WITHOUT THINKING	① ② ③ ④ ⑤ ⑥ ⑦ ⑧ ⑨ ⑩
INTERRUPTING OTHERS	① ② ③ ④ ⑤ ⑥ ⑦ ⑧ ⑨ ⑩
EASILY FRUSTRATED	① ② ③ ④ ⑤ ⑥ ⑦ ⑧ ⑨ ⑩
UNABLE TO HOLD BACKE MOTIONS	① ② ③ ④ ⑤ ⑥ ⑦ ⑧ ⑨ ⑩

MEALS

MEDICATIONS

WATER TRACKER

NOTES

....
....

DAY GOALS

1 ....
2 ....
3 ....

DATE

WEEK

LOCATION

WEIGHT

MOOD TRACKER

BEHAVIOR

INATTENTION

SHORT ATTENTION	① ② ③ ④ ⑤ ⑥ ⑦ ⑧ ⑨ ⑩
UNMOTIVATED / BORED	① ② ③ ④ ⑤ ⑥ ⑦ ⑧ ⑨ ⑩
SHORT ATTENTION	① ② ③ ④ ⑤ ⑥ ⑦ ⑧ ⑨ ⑩
FORGETFUL / CONFUSIONED	① ② ③ ④ ⑤ ⑥ ⑦ ⑧ ⑨ ⑩

HYPERACTIVITY

CONSTANTLY MOVING / TALKING	① ② ③ ④ ⑤ ⑥ ⑦ ⑧ ⑨ ⑩
STRUGGLING TO SIT STILL	① ② ③ ④ ⑤ ⑥ ⑦ ⑧ ⑨ ⑩
TOUCHING THINGS REPEATEDLY	① ② ③ ④ ⑤ ⑥ ⑦ ⑧ ⑨ ⑩
DIFFICULT SLEEPING	① ② ③ ④ ⑤ ⑥ ⑦ ⑧ ⑨ ⑩

IMPULSIVITY

ACTING WITHOUT THINKING	① ② ③ ④ ⑤ ⑥ ⑦ ⑧ ⑨ ⑩
INTERRUPTING OTHERS	① ② ③ ④ ⑤ ⑥ ⑦ ⑧ ⑨ ⑩
EASILY FRUSTRATED	① ② ③ ④ ⑤ ⑥ ⑦ ⑧ ⑨ ⑩
UNABLE TO HOLD BACKE MOTIONS	① ② ③ ④ ⑤ ⑥ ⑦ ⑧ ⑨ ⑩

MEALS

MEDICATIONS

WATER TRACKER

NOTES

....
....

DAY GOALS

1 ....
2 ....
3 ....

DATE
WEEK
LOCATION
WEIGHT

MOOD TRACKER

BEHAVIOR

INATTENTION

SHORT ATTENTION	① ② ③ ④ ⑤ ⑥ ⑦ ⑧ ⑨ ⑩
UNMOTIVATED / BORED	① ② ③ ④ ⑤ ⑥ ⑦ ⑧ ⑨ ⑩
SHORT ATTENTION	① ② ③ ④ ⑤ ⑥ ⑦ ⑧ ⑨ ⑩
FORGETFUL / CONFUSIONED	① ② ③ ④ ⑤ ⑥ ⑦ ⑧ ⑨ ⑩

HYPERACTIVITY

CONSTANTLY MOVING / TALKING	① ② ③ ④ ⑤ ⑥ ⑦ ⑧ ⑨ ⑩
STRUGGLING TO SIT STILL	① ② ③ ④ ⑤ ⑥ ⑦ ⑧ ⑨ ⑩
TOUCHING THINGS REPEATEDLY	① ② ③ ④ ⑤ ⑥ ⑦ ⑧ ⑨ ⑩
DIFFICULT SLEEPING	① ② ③ ④ ⑤ ⑥ ⑦ ⑧ ⑨ ⑩

IMPULSIVITY

ACTING WITHOUT THINKING	① ② ③ ④ ⑤ ⑥ ⑦ ⑧ ⑨ ⑩
INTERRUPTING OTHERS	① ② ③ ④ ⑤ ⑥ ⑦ ⑧ ⑨ ⑩
EASILY FRUSTRATED	① ② ③ ④ ⑤ ⑥ ⑦ ⑧ ⑨ ⑩
UNABLE TO HOLD BACKE MOTIONS	① ② ③ ④ ⑤ ⑥ ⑦ ⑧ ⑨ ⑩

MEALS

MEDICATIONS

WATER TRACKER

NOTES

....
....

DAY GOALS

1 ....
2 ....
3 ....

DATE
WEEK
LOCATION
WEIGHT

MOOD TRACKER

BEHAVIOR

INATTENTION

SHORT ATTENTION	① ② ③ ④ ⑤ ⑥ ⑦ ⑧ ⑨ ⑩
UNMOTIVATED / BORED	① ② ③ ④ ⑤ ⑥ ⑦ ⑧ ⑨ ⑩
SHORT ATTENTION	① ② ③ ④ ⑤ ⑥ ⑦ ⑧ ⑨ ⑩
FORGETFUL / CONFUSIONED	① ② ③ ④ ⑤ ⑥ ⑦ ⑧ ⑨ ⑩

HYPERACTIVITY

CONSTANTLY MOVING / TALKING	① ② ③ ④ ⑤ ⑥ ⑦ ⑧ ⑨ ⑩
STRUGGLING TO SIT STILL	① ② ③ ④ ⑤ ⑥ ⑦ ⑧ ⑨ ⑩
TOUCHING THINGS REPEATEDLY	① ② ③ ④ ⑤ ⑥ ⑦ ⑧ ⑨ ⑩
DIFFICULT SLEEPING	① ② ③ ④ ⑤ ⑥ ⑦ ⑧ ⑨ ⑩

IMPULSIVITY

ACTING WITHOUT THINKING	① ② ③ ④ ⑤ ⑥ ⑦ ⑧ ⑨ ⑩
INTERRUPTING OTHERS	① ② ③ ④ ⑤ ⑥ ⑦ ⑧ ⑨ ⑩
EASILY FRUSTRATED	① ② ③ ④ ⑤ ⑥ ⑦ ⑧ ⑨ ⑩
UNABLE TO HOLD BACKE MOTIONS	① ② ③ ④ ⑤ ⑥ ⑦ ⑧ ⑨ ⑩

MEALS

MEDICATIONS

WATER TRACKER

NOTES

....
....

DAY GOALS

1 ....
2 ....
3 ....

DATE

WEEK

LOCATION

WEIGHT

MOOD TRACKER

BEHAVIOR

INATTENTION

SHORT ATTENTION	① ② ③ ④ ⑤ ⑥ ⑦ ⑧ ⑨ ⑩
UNMOTIVATED / BORED	① ② ③ ④ ⑤ ⑥ ⑦ ⑧ ⑨ ⑩
SHORT ATTENTION	① ② ③ ④ ⑤ ⑥ ⑦ ⑧ ⑨ ⑩
FORGETFUL / CONFUSIONED	① ② ③ ④ ⑤ ⑥ ⑦ ⑧ ⑨ ⑩

HYPERACTIVITY

CONSTANTLY MOVING / TALKING	① ② ③ ④ ⑤ ⑥ ⑦ ⑧ ⑨ ⑩
STRUGGLING TO SIT STILL	① ② ③ ④ ⑤ ⑥ ⑦ ⑧ ⑨ ⑩
TOUCHING THINGS REPEATEDLY	① ② ③ ④ ⑤ ⑥ ⑦ ⑧ ⑨ ⑩
DIFFICULT SLEEPING	① ② ③ ④ ⑤ ⑥ ⑦ ⑧ ⑨ ⑩

IMPULSIVITY

ACTING WITHOUT THINKING	① ② ③ ④ ⑤ ⑥ ⑦ ⑧ ⑨ ⑩
INTERRUPTING OTHERS	① ② ③ ④ ⑤ ⑥ ⑦ ⑧ ⑨ ⑩
EASILY FRUSTRATED	① ② ③ ④ ⑤ ⑥ ⑦ ⑧ ⑨ ⑩
UNABLE TO HOLD BACKE MOTIONS	① ② ③ ④ ⑤ ⑥ ⑦ ⑧ ⑨ ⑩

MEALS

MEDICATIONS

WATER TRACKER

NOTES

....
....

1 ....
2 ....
3 ....

DATE
WEEK
LOCATION
WEIGHT

MOOD TRACKER

BEHAVIOR

INATTENTION

SHORT ATTENTION	① ② ③ ④ ⑤ ⑥ ⑦ ⑧ ⑨ ⑩
UNMOTIVATED / BORED	① ② ③ ④ ⑤ ⑥ ⑦ ⑧ ⑨ ⑩
SHORT ATTENTION	① ② ③ ④ ⑤ ⑥ ⑦ ⑧ ⑨ ⑩
FORGETFUL / CONFUSIONED	① ② ③ ④ ⑤ ⑥ ⑦ ⑧ ⑨ ⑩

HYPERACTIVITY

CONSTANTLY MOVING / TALKING	① ② ③ ④ ⑤ ⑥ ⑦ ⑧ ⑨ ⑩
STRUGGLING TO SIT STILL	① ② ③ ④ ⑤ ⑥ ⑦ ⑧ ⑨ ⑩
TOUCHING THINGS REPEATEDLY	① ② ③ ④ ⑤ ⑥ ⑦ ⑧ ⑨ ⑩
DIFFICULT SLEEPING	① ② ③ ④ ⑤ ⑥ ⑦ ⑧ ⑨ ⑩

IMPULSIVITY

ACTING WITHOUT THINKING	① ② ③ ④ ⑤ ⑥ ⑦ ⑧ ⑨ ⑩
INTERRUPTING OTHERS	① ② ③ ④ ⑤ ⑥ ⑦ ⑧ ⑨ ⑩
EASILY FRUSTRATED	① ② ③ ④ ⑤ ⑥ ⑦ ⑧ ⑨ ⑩
UNABLE TO HOLD BACKE MOTIONS	① ② ③ ④ ⑤ ⑥ ⑦ ⑧ ⑨ ⑩

MEALS

MEDICATIONS

WATER TRACKER

NOTES

....
....

DAY GOALS

1 ....
2 ....
3 ....

DATE

WEEK

LOCATION

WEIGHT

MOOD TRACKER :(:| >< :(>:(:D

BEHAVIOR

INATTENTION

SHORT ATTENTION	① ② ③ ④ ⑤ ⑥ ⑦ ⑧ ⑨ ⑩
UNMOTIVATED / BORED	① ② ③ ④ ⑤ ⑥ ⑦ ⑧ ⑨ ⑩
SHORT ATTENTION	① ② ③ ④ ⑤ ⑥ ⑦ ⑧ ⑨ ⑩
FORGETFUL / CONFUSIONED	① ② ③ ④ ⑤ ⑥ ⑦ ⑧ ⑨ ⑩

HYPERACTIVITY

CONSTANTLY MOVING / TALKING	① ② ③ ④ ⑤ ⑥ ⑦ ⑧ ⑨ ⑩
STRUGGLING TO SIT STILL	① ② ③ ④ ⑤ ⑥ ⑦ ⑧ ⑨ ⑩
TOUCHING THINGS REPEATEDLY	① ② ③ ④ ⑤ ⑥ ⑦ ⑧ ⑨ ⑩
DIFFICULT SLEEPING	① ② ③ ④ ⑤ ⑥ ⑦ ⑧ ⑨ ⑩

IMPULSIVITY

ACTING WITHOUT THINKING	① ② ③ ④ ⑤ ⑥ ⑦ ⑧ ⑨ ⑩
INTERRUPTING OTHERS	① ② ③ ④ ⑤ ⑥ ⑦ ⑧ ⑨ ⑩
EASILY FRUSTRATED	① ② ③ ④ ⑤ ⑥ ⑦ ⑧ ⑨ ⑩
UNABLE TO HOLD BACKE MOTIONS	① ② ③ ④ ⑤ ⑥ ⑦ ⑧ ⑨ ⑩

MEALS

MEDICATIONS

WATER TRACKER ⎕ ⎕ ⎕ ⎕ ⎕ ⎕ ⎕

NOTES

....
....

MOOD TRACKER

BEHAVIOR

INATTENTION

SHORT ATTENTION	(1)(2)(3)(4)(5)(6)(7)(8)(9)(10)
UNMOTIVATED / BORED	(1)(2)(3)(4)(5)(6)(7)(8)(9)(10)
SHORT ATTENTION	(1)(2)(3)(4)(5)(6)(7)(8)(9)(10)
FORGETFUL / CONFUSIONED	(1)(2)(3)(4)(5)(6)(7)(8)(9)(10)

HYPERACTIVITY

CONSTANTLY MOVING / TALKING	(1)(2)(3)(4)(5)(6)(7)(8)(9)(10)
STRUGGLING TO SIT STILL	(1)(2)(3)(4)(5)(6)(7)(8)(9)(10)
TOUCHING THINGS REPEATEDLY	(1)(2)(3)(4)(5)(6)(7)(8)(9)(10)
DIFFICULT SLEEPING	(1)(2)(3)(4)(5)(6)(7)(8)(9)(10)

IMPULSIVITY

ACTING WITHOUT THINKING	(1)(2)(3)(4)(5)(6)(7)(8)(9)(10)
INTERRUPTING OTHERS	(1)(2)(3)(4)(5)(6)(7)(8)(9)(10)
EASILY FRUSTRATED	(1)(2)(3)(4)(5)(6)(7)(8)(9)(10)
UNABLE TO HOLD BACKE MOTIONS	(1)(2)(3)(4)(5)(6)(7)(8)(9)(10)

MEALS	MEDICATIONS

WATER TRACKER

NOTES

....
....

DAY GOALS

1 ....
2 ....
3 ....

DATE

WEEK

LOCATION

WEIGHT

MOOD TRACKER

BEHAVIOR

INATTENTION

SHORT ATTENTION	(1)(2)(3)(4)(5)(6)(7)(8)(9)(10)
UNMOTIVATED / BORED	(1)(2)(3)(4)(5)(6)(7)(8)(9)(10)
SHORT ATTENTION	(1)(2)(3)(4)(5)(6)(7)(8)(9)(10)
FORGETFUL / CONFUSIONED	(1)(2)(3)(4)(5)(6)(7)(8)(9)(10)

HYPERACTIVITY

CONSTANTLY MOVING / TALKING	(1)(2)(3)(4)(5)(6)(7)(8)(9)(10)
STRUGGLING TO SIT STILL	(1)(2)(3)(4)(5)(6)(7)(8)(9)(10)
TOUCHING THINGS REPEATEDLY	(1)(2)(3)(4)(5)(6)(7)(8)(9)(10)
DIFFICULT SLEEPING	(1)(2)(3)(4)(5)(6)(7)(8)(9)(10)

IMPULSIVITY

ACTING WITHOUT THINKING	(1)(2)(3)(4)(5)(6)(7)(8)(9)(10)
INTERRUPTING OTHERS	(1)(2)(3)(4)(5)(6)(7)(8)(9)(10)
EASILY FRUSTRATED	(1)(2)(3)(4)(5)(6)(7)(8)(9)(10)
UNABLE TO HOLD BACKE MOTIONS	(1)(2)(3)(4)(5)(6)(7)(8)(9)(10)

MEALS

MEDICATIONS

WATER TRACKER

NOTES

....
....

DAY GOALS

1 ....
2 ....
3 ....

DATE
WEEK
LOCATION
WEIGHT

MOOD TRACKER

:(:| >< :'(>:(:D

BEHAVIOR

INATTENTION

SHORT ATTENTION	① ② ③ ④ ⑤ ⑥ ⑦ ⑧ ⑨ ⑩
UNMOTIVATED / BORED	① ② ③ ④ ⑤ ⑥ ⑦ ⑧ ⑨ ⑩
SHORT ATTENTION	① ② ③ ④ ⑤ ⑥ ⑦ ⑧ ⑨ ⑩
FORGETFUL / CONFUSIONED	① ② ③ ④ ⑤ ⑥ ⑦ ⑧ ⑨ ⑩

HYPERACTIVITY

CONSTANTLY MOVING / TALKING	① ② ③ ④ ⑤ ⑥ ⑦ ⑧ ⑨ ⑩
STRUGGLING TO SIT STILL	① ② ③ ④ ⑤ ⑥ ⑦ ⑧ ⑨ ⑩
TOUCHING THINGS REPEATEDLY	① ② ③ ④ ⑤ ⑥ ⑦ ⑧ ⑨ ⑩
DIFFICULT SLEEPING	① ② ③ ④ ⑤ ⑥ ⑦ ⑧ ⑨ ⑩

IMPULSIVITY

ACTING WITHOUT THINKING	① ② ③ ④ ⑤ ⑥ ⑦ ⑧ ⑨ ⑩
INTERRUPTING OTHERS	① ② ③ ④ ⑤ ⑥ ⑦ ⑧ ⑨ ⑩
EASILY FRUSTRATED	① ② ③ ④ ⑤ ⑥ ⑦ ⑧ ⑨ ⑩
UNABLE TO HOLD BACKE MOTIONS	① ② ③ ④ ⑤ ⑥ ⑦ ⑧ ⑨ ⑩

MEALS

MEDICATIONS

WATER TRACKER

NOTES

....
....

DAY GOALS

1 ....
2 ....
3 ....

DATE

WEEK

LOCATION

WEIGHT

MOOD TRACKER

BEHAVIOR

INATTENTION

SHORT ATTENTION	① ② ③ ④ ⑤ ⑥ ⑦ ⑧ ⑨ ⑩
UNMOTIVATED / BORED	① ② ③ ④ ⑤ ⑥ ⑦ ⑧ ⑨ ⑩
SHORT ATTENTION	① ② ③ ④ ⑤ ⑥ ⑦ ⑧ ⑨ ⑩
FORGETFUL / CONFUSIONED	① ② ③ ④ ⑤ ⑥ ⑦ ⑧ ⑨ ⑩

HYPERACTIVITY

CONSTANTLY MOVING / TALKING	① ② ③ ④ ⑤ ⑥ ⑦ ⑧ ⑨ ⑩
STRUGGLING TO SIT STILL	① ② ③ ④ ⑤ ⑥ ⑦ ⑧ ⑨ ⑩
TOUCHING THINGS REPEATEDLY	① ② ③ ④ ⑤ ⑥ ⑦ ⑧ ⑨ ⑩
DIFFICULT SLEEPING	① ② ③ ④ ⑤ ⑥ ⑦ ⑧ ⑨ ⑩

IMPULSIVITY

ACTING WITHOUT THINKING	① ② ③ ④ ⑤ ⑥ ⑦ ⑧ ⑨ ⑩
INTERRUPTING OTHERS	① ② ③ ④ ⑤ ⑥ ⑦ ⑧ ⑨ ⑩
EASILY FRUSTRATED	① ② ③ ④ ⑤ ⑥ ⑦ ⑧ ⑨ ⑩
UNABLE TO HOLD BACKE MOTIONS	① ② ③ ④ ⑤ ⑥ ⑦ ⑧ ⑨ ⑩

MEALS

MEDICATIONS

WATER TRACKER

NOTES

....
....

MOOD TRACKER

BEHAVIOR

INATTENTION

SHORT ATTENTION	① ② ③ ④ ⑤ ⑥ ⑦ ⑧ ⑨ ⑩
UNMOTIVATED / BORED	① ② ③ ④ ⑤ ⑥ ⑦ ⑧ ⑨ ⑩
SHORT ATTENTION	① ② ③ ④ ⑤ ⑥ ⑦ ⑧ ⑨ ⑩
FORGETFUL / CONFUSIONED	① ② ③ ④ ⑤ ⑥ ⑦ ⑧ ⑨ ⑩

HYPERACTIVITY

CONSTANTLY MOVING / TALKING	① ② ③ ④ ⑤ ⑥ ⑦ ⑧ ⑨ ⑩
STRUGGLING TO SIT STILL	① ② ③ ④ ⑤ ⑥ ⑦ ⑧ ⑨ ⑩
TOUCHING THINGS REPEATEDLY	① ② ③ ④ ⑤ ⑥ ⑦ ⑧ ⑨ ⑩
DIFFICULT SLEEPING	① ② ③ ④ ⑤ ⑥ ⑦ ⑧ ⑨ ⑩

IMPULSIVITY

ACTING WITHOUT THINKING	① ② ③ ④ ⑤ ⑥ ⑦ ⑧ ⑨ ⑩
INTERRUPTING OTHERS	① ② ③ ④ ⑤ ⑥ ⑦ ⑧ ⑨ ⑩
EASILY FRUSTRATED	① ② ③ ④ ⑤ ⑥ ⑦ ⑧ ⑨ ⑩
UNABLE TO HOLD BACKE MOTIONS	① ② ③ ④ ⑤ ⑥ ⑦ ⑧ ⑨ ⑩

MEALS	MEDICATIONS

WATER TRACKER

NOTES

....
....

DAY GOALS

1 ....
2 ....
3 ....

DATE
WEEK
LOCATION
WEIGHT

MOOD TRACKER

BEHAVIOR

INATTENTION

SHORT ATTENTION	① ② ③ ④ ⑤ ⑥ ⑦ ⑧ ⑨ ⑩
UNMOTIVATED / BORED	① ② ③ ④ ⑤ ⑥ ⑦ ⑧ ⑨ ⑩
SHORT ATTENTION	① ② ③ ④ ⑤ ⑥ ⑦ ⑧ ⑨ ⑩
FORGETFUL / CONFUSIONED	① ② ③ ④ ⑤ ⑥ ⑦ ⑧ ⑨ ⑩

HYPERACTIVITY

CONSTANTLY MOVING / TALKING	① ② ③ ④ ⑤ ⑥ ⑦ ⑧ ⑨ ⑩
STRUGGLING TO SIT STILL	① ② ③ ④ ⑤ ⑥ ⑦ ⑧ ⑨ ⑩
TOUCHING THINGS REPEATEDLY	① ② ③ ④ ⑤ ⑥ ⑦ ⑧ ⑨ ⑩
DIFFICULT SLEEPING	① ② ③ ④ ⑤ ⑥ ⑦ ⑧ ⑨ ⑩

IMPULSIVITY

ACTING WITHOUT THINKING	① ② ③ ④ ⑤ ⑥ ⑦ ⑧ ⑨ ⑩
INTERRUPTING OTHERS	① ② ③ ④ ⑤ ⑥ ⑦ ⑧ ⑨ ⑩
EASILY FRUSTRATED	① ② ③ ④ ⑤ ⑥ ⑦ ⑧ ⑨ ⑩
UNABLE TO HOLD BACKE MOTIONS	① ② ③ ④ ⑤ ⑥ ⑦ ⑧ ⑨ ⑩

MEALS

MEDICATIONS

WATER TRACKER

NOTES

....
....

1 ....
2 ....
3 ....

DATE
WEEK
LOCATION
WEIGHT

MOOD TRACKER

BEHAVIOR

INATTENTION

SHORT ATTENTION	① ② ③ ④ ⑤ ⑥ ⑦ ⑧ ⑨ ⑩
UNMOTIVATED / BORED	① ② ③ ④ ⑤ ⑥ ⑦ ⑧ ⑨ ⑩
SHORT ATTENTION	① ② ③ ④ ⑤ ⑥ ⑦ ⑧ ⑨ ⑩
FORGETFUL / CONFUSIONED	① ② ③ ④ ⑤ ⑥ ⑦ ⑧ ⑨ ⑩

HYPERACTIVITY

CONSTANTLY MOVING / TALKING	① ② ③ ④ ⑤ ⑥ ⑦ ⑧ ⑨ ⑩
STRUGGLING TO SIT STILL	① ② ③ ④ ⑤ ⑥ ⑦ ⑧ ⑨ ⑩
TOUCHING THINGS REPEATEDLY	① ② ③ ④ ⑤ ⑥ ⑦ ⑧ ⑨ ⑩
DIFFICULT SLEEPING	① ② ③ ④ ⑤ ⑥ ⑦ ⑧ ⑨ ⑩

IMPULSIVITY

ACTING WITHOUT THINKING	① ② ③ ④ ⑤ ⑥ ⑦ ⑧ ⑨ ⑩
INTERRUPTING OTHERS	① ② ③ ④ ⑤ ⑥ ⑦ ⑧ ⑨ ⑩
EASILY FRUSTRATED	① ② ③ ④ ⑤ ⑥ ⑦ ⑧ ⑨ ⑩
UNABLE TO HOLD BACKE MOTIONS	① ② ③ ④ ⑤ ⑥ ⑦ ⑧ ⑨ ⑩

MEALS

MEDICATIONS

WATER TRACKER

NOTES

....
....

DAY GOALS

1 ....
2 ....
3 ....

DATE

WEEK

LOCATION

WEIGHT

MOOD TRACKER

:-(:-| >< :-(>:(:-D

BEHAVIOR

INATTENTION

SHORT ATTENTION	① ② ③ ④ ⑤ ⑥ ⑦ ⑧ ⑨ ⑩
UNMOTIVATED / BORED	① ② ③ ④ ⑤ ⑥ ⑦ ⑧ ⑨ ⑩
SHORT ATTENTION	① ② ③ ④ ⑤ ⑥ ⑦ ⑧ ⑨ ⑩
FORGETFUL / CONFUSIONED	① ② ③ ④ ⑤ ⑥ ⑦ ⑧ ⑨ ⑩

HYPERACTIVITY

CONSTANTLY MOVING / TALKING	① ② ③ ④ ⑤ ⑥ ⑦ ⑧ ⑨ ⑩
STRUGGLING TO SIT STILL	① ② ③ ④ ⑤ ⑥ ⑦ ⑧ ⑨ ⑩
TOUCHING THINGS REPEATEDLY	① ② ③ ④ ⑤ ⑥ ⑦ ⑧ ⑨ ⑩
DIFFICULT SLEEPING	① ② ③ ④ ⑤ ⑥ ⑦ ⑧ ⑨ ⑩

IMPULSIVITY

ACTING WITHOUT THINKING	① ② ③ ④ ⑤ ⑥ ⑦ ⑧ ⑨ ⑩
INTERRUPTING OTHERS	① ② ③ ④ ⑤ ⑥ ⑦ ⑧ ⑨ ⑩
EASILY FRUSTRATED	① ② ③ ④ ⑤ ⑥ ⑦ ⑧ ⑨ ⑩
UNABLE TO HOLD BACKE MOTIONS	① ② ③ ④ ⑤ ⑥ ⑦ ⑧ ⑨ ⑩

MEALS

MEDICATIONS

WATER TRACKER

NOTES

....
....

1 ....
2 ....
3 ....

DATE
WEEK
LOCATION
WEIGHT

MOOD TRACKER

BEHAVIOR

INATTENTION

SHORT ATTENTION	(1)(2)(3)(4)(5)(6)(7)(8)(9)(10)
UNMOTIVATED / BORED	(1)(2)(3)(4)(5)(6)(7)(8)(9)(10)
SHORT ATTENTION	(1)(2)(3)(4)(5)(6)(7)(8)(9)(10)
FORGETFUL / CONFUSIONED	(1)(2)(3)(4)(5)(6)(7)(8)(9)(10)

HYPERACTIVITY

CONSTANTLY MOVING / TALKING	(1)(2)(3)(4)(5)(6)(7)(8)(9)(10)
STRUGGLING TO SIT STILL	(1)(2)(3)(4)(5)(6)(7)(8)(9)(10)
TOUCHING THINGS REPEATEDLY	(1)(2)(3)(4)(5)(6)(7)(8)(9)(10)
DIFFICULT SLEEPING	(1)(2)(3)(4)(5)(6)(7)(8)(9)(10)

IMPULSIVITY

ACTING WITHOUT THINKING	(1)(2)(3)(4)(5)(6)(7)(8)(9)(10)
INTERRUPTING OTHERS	(1)(2)(3)(4)(5)(6)(7)(8)(9)(10)
EASILY FRUSTRATED	(1)(2)(3)(4)(5)(6)(7)(8)(9)(10)
UNABLE TO HOLD BACKE MOTIONS	(1)(2)(3)(4)(5)(6)(7)(8)(9)(10)

MEALS

MEDICATIONS

WATER TRACKER

NOTES

....
....

DAY GOALS

1 ....
2 ....
3 ....

DATE

WEEK

LOCATION

WEIGHT

MOOD TRACKER

BEHAVIOR

INATTENTION

SHORT ATTENTION	① ② ③ ④ ⑤ ⑥ ⑦ ⑧ ⑨ ⑩
UNMOTIVATED / BORED	① ② ③ ④ ⑤ ⑥ ⑦ ⑧ ⑨ ⑩
SHORT ATTENTION	① ② ③ ④ ⑤ ⑥ ⑦ ⑧ ⑨ ⑩
FORGETFUL / CONFUSIONED	① ② ③ ④ ⑤ ⑥ ⑦ ⑧ ⑨ ⑩

HYPERACTIVITY

CONSTANTLY MOVING / TALKING	① ② ③ ④ ⑤ ⑥ ⑦ ⑧ ⑨ ⑩
STRUGGLING TO SIT STILL	① ② ③ ④ ⑤ ⑥ ⑦ ⑧ ⑨ ⑩
TOUCHING THINGS REPEATEDLY	① ② ③ ④ ⑤ ⑥ ⑦ ⑧ ⑨ ⑩
DIFFICULT SLEEPING	① ② ③ ④ ⑤ ⑥ ⑦ ⑧ ⑨ ⑩

IMPULSIVITY

ACTING WITHOUT THINKING	① ② ③ ④ ⑤ ⑥ ⑦ ⑧ ⑨ ⑩
INTERRUPTING OTHERS	① ② ③ ④ ⑤ ⑥ ⑦ ⑧ ⑨ ⑩
EASILY FRUSTRATED	① ② ③ ④ ⑤ ⑥ ⑦ ⑧ ⑨ ⑩
UNABLE TO HOLD BACKE MOTIONS	① ② ③ ④ ⑤ ⑥ ⑦ ⑧ ⑨ ⑩

MEALS

MEDICATIONS

WATER TRACKER

NOTES

....
....

DAY GOALS

1 ....
2 ....
3 ....

DATE

WEEK

LOCATION

WEIGHT

MOOD TRACKER 😕 😐 😣 🙁 😠 😃

BEHAVIOR

INATTENTION

SHORT ATTENTION	① ② ③ ④ ⑤ ⑥ ⑦ ⑧ ⑨ ⑩
UNMOTIVATED / BORED	① ② ③ ④ ⑤ ⑥ ⑦ ⑧ ⑨ ⑩
SHORT ATTENTION	① ② ③ ④ ⑤ ⑥ ⑦ ⑧ ⑨ ⑩
FORGETFUL / CONFUSIONED	① ② ③ ④ ⑤ ⑥ ⑦ ⑧ ⑨ ⑩

HYPERACTIVITY

CONSTANTLY MOVING / TALKING	① ② ③ ④ ⑤ ⑥ ⑦ ⑧ ⑨ ⑩
STRUGGLING TO SIT STILL	① ② ③ ④ ⑤ ⑥ ⑦ ⑧ ⑨ ⑩
TOUCHING THINGS REPEATEDLY	① ② ③ ④ ⑤ ⑥ ⑦ ⑧ ⑨ ⑩
DIFFICULT SLEEPING	① ② ③ ④ ⑤ ⑥ ⑦ ⑧ ⑨ ⑩

IMPULSIVITY

ACTING WITHOUT THINKING	① ② ③ ④ ⑤ ⑥ ⑦ ⑧ ⑨ ⑩
INTERRUPTING OTHERS	① ② ③ ④ ⑤ ⑥ ⑦ ⑧ ⑨ ⑩
EASILY FRUSTRATED	① ② ③ ④ ⑤ ⑥ ⑦ ⑧ ⑨ ⑩
UNABLE TO HOLD BACKE MOTIONS	① ② ③ ④ ⑤ ⑥ ⑦ ⑧ ⑨ ⑩

MEALS

MEDICATIONS

WATER TRACKER 🥤 🥤 🥤 🥤 🥤 🥤 🥤

NOTES

....
....

DAY GOALS

1 ....
2 ....
3 ....

DATE

WEEK

LOCATION

WEIGHT

MOOD TRACKER

BEHAVIOR

INATTENTION

SHORT ATTENTION	(1)(2)(3)(4)(5)(6)(7)(8)(9)(10)
UNMOTIVATED / BORED	(1)(2)(3)(4)(5)(6)(7)(8)(9)(10)
SHORT ATTENTION	(1)(2)(3)(4)(5)(6)(7)(8)(9)(10)
FORGETFUL / CONFUSIONED	(1)(2)(3)(4)(5)(6)(7)(8)(9)(10)

HYPERACTIVITY

CONSTANTLY MOVING / TALKING	(1)(2)(3)(4)(5)(6)(7)(8)(9)(10)
STRUGGLING TO SIT STILL	(1)(2)(3)(4)(5)(6)(7)(8)(9)(10)
TOUCHING THINGS REPEATEDLY	(1)(2)(3)(4)(5)(6)(7)(8)(9)(10)
DIFFICULT SLEEPING	(1)(2)(3)(4)(5)(6)(7)(8)(9)(10)

IMPULSIVITY

ACTING WITHOUT THINKING	(1)(2)(3)(4)(5)(6)(7)(8)(9)(10)
INTERRUPTING OTHERS	(1)(2)(3)(4)(5)(6)(7)(8)(9)(10)
EASILY FRUSTRATED	(1)(2)(3)(4)(5)(6)(7)(8)(9)(10)
UNABLE TO HOLD BACKE MOTIONS	(1)(2)(3)(4)(5)(6)(7)(8)(9)(10)

MEALS

MEDICATIONS

WATER TRACKER

NOTES

....
....

DAY GOALS

1 ....
2 ....
3 ....

DATE
WEEK
LOCATION
WEIGHT

MOOD TRACKER

BEHAVIOR

INATTENTION

SHORT ATTENTION	① ② ③ ④ ⑤ ⑥ ⑦ ⑧ ⑨ ⑩
UNMOTIVATED / BORED	① ② ③ ④ ⑤ ⑥ ⑦ ⑧ ⑨ ⑩
SHORT ATTENTION	① ② ③ ④ ⑤ ⑥ ⑦ ⑧ ⑨ ⑩
FORGETFUL / CONFUSIONED	① ② ③ ④ ⑤ ⑥ ⑦ ⑧ ⑨ ⑩

HYPERACTIVITY

CONSTANTLY MOVING / TALKING	① ② ③ ④ ⑤ ⑥ ⑦ ⑧ ⑨ ⑩
STRUGGLING TO SIT STILL	① ② ③ ④ ⑤ ⑥ ⑦ ⑧ ⑨ ⑩
TOUCHING THINGS REPEATEDLY	① ② ③ ④ ⑤ ⑥ ⑦ ⑧ ⑨ ⑩
DIFFICULT SLEEPING	① ② ③ ④ ⑤ ⑥ ⑦ ⑧ ⑨ ⑩

IMPULSIVITY

ACTING WITHOUT THINKING	① ② ③ ④ ⑤ ⑥ ⑦ ⑧ ⑨ ⑩
INTERRUPTING OTHERS	① ② ③ ④ ⑤ ⑥ ⑦ ⑧ ⑨ ⑩
EASILY FRUSTRATED	① ② ③ ④ ⑤ ⑥ ⑦ ⑧ ⑨ ⑩
UNABLE TO HOLD BACKE MOTIONS	① ② ③ ④ ⑤ ⑥ ⑦ ⑧ ⑨ ⑩

MEALS

MEDICATIONS

WATER TRACKER

NOTES

....
....

DAY GOALS

1 ....
2 ....
3 ....

DATE

WEEK

LOCATION

WEIGHT

MOOD TRACKER

BEHAVIOR

INATTENTION

SHORT ATTENTION — ① ② ③ ④ ⑤ ⑥ ⑦ ⑧ ⑨ ⑩

UNMOTIVATED / BORED — ① ② ③ ④ ⑤ ⑥ ⑦ ⑧ ⑨ ⑩

SHORT ATTENTION — ① ② ③ ④ ⑤ ⑥ ⑦ ⑧ ⑨ ⑩

FORGETFUL / CONFUSIONED — ① ② ③ ④ ⑤ ⑥ ⑦ ⑧ ⑨ ⑩

HYPERACTIVITY

CONSTANTLY MOVING / TALKING — ① ② ③ ④ ⑤ ⑥ ⑦ ⑧ ⑨ ⑩

STRUGGLING TO SIT STILL — ① ② ③ ④ ⑤ ⑥ ⑦ ⑧ ⑨ ⑩

TOUCHING THINGS REPEATEDLY — ① ② ③ ④ ⑤ ⑥ ⑦ ⑧ ⑨ ⑩

DIFFICULT SLEEPING — ① ② ③ ④ ⑤ ⑥ ⑦ ⑧ ⑨ ⑩

IMPULSIVITY

ACTING WITHOUT THINKING — ① ② ③ ④ ⑤ ⑥ ⑦ ⑧ ⑨ ⑩

INTERRUPTING OTHERS — ① ② ③ ④ ⑤ ⑥ ⑦ ⑧ ⑨ ⑩

EASILY FRUSTRATED — ① ② ③ ④ ⑤ ⑥ ⑦ ⑧ ⑨ ⑩

UNABLE TO HOLD BACKE MOTIONS — ① ② ③ ④ ⑤ ⑥ ⑦ ⑧ ⑨ ⑩

MEALS

MEDICATIONS

WATER TRACKER

NOTES

....
....

DAY GOALS

1 ....
2 ....
3 ....

DATE
WEEK
LOCATION
WEIGHT

MOOD TRACKER

BEHAVIOR

INATTENTION

SHORT ATTENTION	①②③④⑤⑥⑦⑧⑨⑩
UNMOTIVATED / BORED	①②③④⑤⑥⑦⑧⑨⑩
SHORT ATTENTION	①②③④⑤⑥⑦⑧⑨⑩
FORGETFUL / CONFUSIONED	①②③④⑤⑥⑦⑧⑨⑩

HYPERACTIVITY

CONSTANTLY MOVING / TALKING	①②③④⑤⑥⑦⑧⑨⑩
STRUGGLING TO SIT STILL	①②③④⑤⑥⑦⑧⑨⑩
TOUCHING THINGS REPEATEDLY	①②③④⑤⑥⑦⑧⑨⑩
DIFFICULT SLEEPING	①②③④⑤⑥⑦⑧⑨⑩

IMPULSIVITY

ACTING WITHOUT THINKING	①②③④⑤⑥⑦⑧⑨⑩
INTERRUPTING OTHERS	①②③④⑤⑥⑦⑧⑨⑩
EASILY FRUSTRATED	①②③④⑤⑥⑦⑧⑨⑩
UNABLE TO HOLD BACKE MOTIONS	①②③④⑤⑥⑦⑧⑨⑩

MEALS

MEDICATIONS

WATER TRACKER

NOTES

....
....

DAY GOALS

1 ....
2 ....
3 ....

DATE

WEEK

LOCATION

WEIGHT

MOOD TRACKER

BEHAVIOR

INATTENTION

SHORT ATTENTION	① ② ③ ④ ⑤ ⑥ ⑦ ⑧ ⑨ ⑩
UNMOTIVATED / BORED	① ② ③ ④ ⑤ ⑥ ⑦ ⑧ ⑨ ⑩
SHORT ATTENTION	① ② ③ ④ ⑤ ⑥ ⑦ ⑧ ⑨ ⑩
FORGETFUL / CONFUSIONED	① ② ③ ④ ⑤ ⑥ ⑦ ⑧ ⑨ ⑩

HYPERACTIVITY

CONSTANTLY MOVING / TALKING	① ② ③ ④ ⑤ ⑥ ⑦ ⑧ ⑨ ⑩
STRUGGLING TO SIT STILL	① ② ③ ④ ⑤ ⑥ ⑦ ⑧ ⑨ ⑩
TOUCHING THINGS REPEATEDLY	① ② ③ ④ ⑤ ⑥ ⑦ ⑧ ⑨ ⑩
DIFFICULT SLEEPING	① ② ③ ④ ⑤ ⑥ ⑦ ⑧ ⑨ ⑩

IMPULSIVITY

ACTING WITHOUT THINKING	① ② ③ ④ ⑤ ⑥ ⑦ ⑧ ⑨ ⑩
INTERRUPTING OTHERS	① ② ③ ④ ⑤ ⑥ ⑦ ⑧ ⑨ ⑩
EASILY FRUSTRATED	① ② ③ ④ ⑤ ⑥ ⑦ ⑧ ⑨ ⑩
UNABLE TO HOLD BACKE MOTIONS	① ② ③ ④ ⑤ ⑥ ⑦ ⑧ ⑨ ⑩

MEALS

MEDICATIONS

WATER TRACKER

NOTES

....
....

DAY GOALS

1 ....
2 ....
3 ....

DATE

WEEK

LOCATION

WEIGHT

MOOD TRACKER

BEHAVIOR

INATTENTION

SHORT ATTENTION	① ② ③ ④ ⑤ ⑥ ⑦ ⑧ ⑨ ⑩
UNMOTIVATED / BORED	① ② ③ ④ ⑤ ⑥ ⑦ ⑧ ⑨ ⑩
SHORT ATTENTION	① ② ③ ④ ⑤ ⑥ ⑦ ⑧ ⑨ ⑩
FORGETFUL / CONFUSIONED	① ② ③ ④ ⑤ ⑥ ⑦ ⑧ ⑨ ⑩

HYPERACTIVITY

CONSTANTLY MOVING / TALKING	① ② ③ ④ ⑤ ⑥ ⑦ ⑧ ⑨ ⑩
STRUGGLING TO SIT STILL	① ② ③ ④ ⑤ ⑥ ⑦ ⑧ ⑨ ⑩
TOUCHING THINGS REPEATEDLY	① ② ③ ④ ⑤ ⑥ ⑦ ⑧ ⑨ ⑩
DIFFICULT SLEEPING	① ② ③ ④ ⑤ ⑥ ⑦ ⑧ ⑨ ⑩

IMPULSIVITY

ACTING WITHOUT THINKING	① ② ③ ④ ⑤ ⑥ ⑦ ⑧ ⑨ ⑩
INTERRUPTING OTHERS	① ② ③ ④ ⑤ ⑥ ⑦ ⑧ ⑨ ⑩
EASILY FRUSTRATED	① ② ③ ④ ⑤ ⑥ ⑦ ⑧ ⑨ ⑩
UNABLE TO HOLD BACKE MOTIONS	① ② ③ ④ ⑤ ⑥ ⑦ ⑧ ⑨ ⑩

MEALS

MEDICATIONS

WATER TRACKER

NOTES

....
....

DAY GOALS

1 ....
2 ....
3 ....

DATE
WEEK
LOCATION
WEIGHT

MOOD TRACKER

BEHAVIOR

INATTENTION

SHORT ATTENTION	① ② ③ ④ ⑤ ⑥ ⑦ ⑧ ⑨ ⑩
UNMOTIVATED / BORED	① ② ③ ④ ⑤ ⑥ ⑦ ⑧ ⑨ ⑩
SHORT ATTENTION	① ② ③ ④ ⑤ ⑥ ⑦ ⑧ ⑨ ⑩
FORGETFUL / CONFUSIONED	① ② ③ ④ ⑤ ⑥ ⑦ ⑧ ⑨ ⑩

HYPERACTIVITY

CONSTANTLY MOVING / TALKING	① ② ③ ④ ⑤ ⑥ ⑦ ⑧ ⑨ ⑩
STRUGGLING TO SIT STILL	① ② ③ ④ ⑤ ⑥ ⑦ ⑧ ⑨ ⑩
TOUCHING THINGS REPEATEDLY	① ② ③ ④ ⑤ ⑥ ⑦ ⑧ ⑨ ⑩
DIFFICULT SLEEPING	① ② ③ ④ ⑤ ⑥ ⑦ ⑧ ⑨ ⑩

IMPULSIVITY

ACTING WITHOUT THINKING	① ② ③ ④ ⑤ ⑥ ⑦ ⑧ ⑨ ⑩
INTERRUPTING OTHERS	① ② ③ ④ ⑤ ⑥ ⑦ ⑧ ⑨ ⑩
EASILY FRUSTRATED	① ② ③ ④ ⑤ ⑥ ⑦ ⑧ ⑨ ⑩
UNABLE TO HOLD BACKE MOTIONS	① ② ③ ④ ⑤ ⑥ ⑦ ⑧ ⑨ ⑩

MEALS

MEDICATIONS

WATER TRACKER

NOTES

....
....

DAY GOALS

1 ....
2 ....
3 ....

DATE

WEEK

LOCATION

WEIGHT

MOOD TRACKER

BEHAVIOR

INATTENTION

SHORT ATTENTION	① ② ③ ④ ⑤ ⑥ ⑦ ⑧ ⑨ ⑩
UNMOTIVATED / BORED	① ② ③ ④ ⑤ ⑥ ⑦ ⑧ ⑨ ⑩
SHORT ATTENTION	① ② ③ ④ ⑤ ⑥ ⑦ ⑧ ⑨ ⑩
FORGETFUL / CONFUSIONED	① ② ③ ④ ⑤ ⑥ ⑦ ⑧ ⑨ ⑩

HYPERACTIVITY

CONSTANTLY MOVING / TALKING	① ② ③ ④ ⑤ ⑥ ⑦ ⑧ ⑨ ⑩
STRUGGLING TO SIT STILL	① ② ③ ④ ⑤ ⑥ ⑦ ⑧ ⑨ ⑩
TOUCHING THINGS REPEATEDLY	① ② ③ ④ ⑤ ⑥ ⑦ ⑧ ⑨ ⑩
DIFFICULT SLEEPING	① ② ③ ④ ⑤ ⑥ ⑦ ⑧ ⑨ ⑩

IMPULSIVITY

ACTING WITHOUT THINKING	① ② ③ ④ ⑤ ⑥ ⑦ ⑧ ⑨ ⑩
INTERRUPTING OTHERS	① ② ③ ④ ⑤ ⑥ ⑦ ⑧ ⑨ ⑩
EASILY FRUSTRATED	① ② ③ ④ ⑤ ⑥ ⑦ ⑧ ⑨ ⑩
UNABLE TO HOLD BACKE MOTIONS	① ② ③ ④ ⑤ ⑥ ⑦ ⑧ ⑨ ⑩

MEALS

MEDICATIONS

WATER TRACKER

NOTES

....
....

DAY GOALS

1 ....
2 ....
3 ....

DATE
WEEK
LOCATION
WEIGHT

MOOD TRACKER

BEHAVIOR

INATTENTION

SHORT ATTENTION	① ② ③ ④ ⑤ ⑥ ⑦ ⑧ ⑨ ⑩
UNMOTIVATED / BORED	① ② ③ ④ ⑤ ⑥ ⑦ ⑧ ⑨ ⑩
SHORT ATTENTION	① ② ③ ④ ⑤ ⑥ ⑦ ⑧ ⑨ ⑩
FORGETFUL / CONFUSIONED	① ② ③ ④ ⑤ ⑥ ⑦ ⑧ ⑨ ⑩

HYPERACTIVITY

CONSTANTLY MOVING / TALKING	① ② ③ ④ ⑤ ⑥ ⑦ ⑧ ⑨ ⑩
STRUGGLING TO SIT STILL	① ② ③ ④ ⑤ ⑥ ⑦ ⑧ ⑨ ⑩
TOUCHING THINGS REPEATEDLY	① ② ③ ④ ⑤ ⑥ ⑦ ⑧ ⑨ ⑩
DIFFICULT SLEEPING	① ② ③ ④ ⑤ ⑥ ⑦ ⑧ ⑨ ⑩

IMPULSIVITY

ACTING WITHOUT THINKING	① ② ③ ④ ⑤ ⑥ ⑦ ⑧ ⑨ ⑩
INTERRUPTING OTHERS	① ② ③ ④ ⑤ ⑥ ⑦ ⑧ ⑨ ⑩
EASILY FRUSTRATED	① ② ③ ④ ⑤ ⑥ ⑦ ⑧ ⑨ ⑩
UNABLE TO HOLD BACKE MOTIONS	① ② ③ ④ ⑤ ⑥ ⑦ ⑧ ⑨ ⑩

MEALS

MEDICATIONS

WATER TRACKER

NOTES

....
....

MOOD TRACKER

$\odot$ $\odot$ $\odot$ $\odot$ $\odot$ $\odot$

BEHAVIOR

INATTENTION

SHORT ATTENTION	① ② ③ ④ ⑤ ⑥ ⑦ ⑧ ⑨ ⑩
UNMOTIVATED / BORED	① ② ③ ④ ⑤ ⑥ ⑦ ⑧ ⑨ ⑩
SHORT ATTENTION	① ② ③ ④ ⑤ ⑥ ⑦ ⑧ ⑨ ⑩
FORGETFUL / CONFUSIONED	① ② ③ ④ ⑤ ⑥ ⑦ ⑧ ⑨ ⑩

HYPERACTIVITY

CONSTANTLY MOVING / TALKING	① ② ③ ④ ⑤ ⑥ ⑦ ⑧ ⑨ ⑩
STRUGGLING TO SIT STILL	① ② ③ ④ ⑤ ⑥ ⑦ ⑧ ⑨ ⑩
TOUCHING THINGS REPEATEDLY	① ② ③ ④ ⑤ ⑥ ⑦ ⑧ ⑨ ⑩
DIFFICULT SLEEPING	① ② ③ ④ ⑤ ⑥ ⑦ ⑧ ⑨ ⑩

IMPULSIVITY

ACTING WITHOUT THINKING	① ② ③ ④ ⑤ ⑥ ⑦ ⑧ ⑨ ⑩
INTERRUPTING OTHERS	① ② ③ ④ ⑤ ⑥ ⑦ ⑧ ⑨ ⑩
EASILY FRUSTRATED	① ② ③ ④ ⑤ ⑥ ⑦ ⑧ ⑨ ⑩
UNABLE TO HOLD BACKE MOTIONS	① ② ③ ④ ⑤ ⑥ ⑦ ⑧ ⑨ ⑩

MEALS

MEDICATIONS

WATER TRACKER

NOTES

....
....

DAY GOALS

1 ....
2 ....
3 ....

DATE

WEEK

LOCATION

WEIGHT

MOOD TRACKER

😔 😐 😣 😢 😠 😁

BEHAVIOR

INATTENTION

SHORT ATTENTION	① ② ③ ④ ⑤ ⑥ ⑦ ⑧ ⑨ ⑩
UNMOTIVATED / BORED	① ② ③ ④ ⑤ ⑥ ⑦ ⑧ ⑨ ⑩
SHORT ATTENTION	① ② ③ ④ ⑤ ⑥ ⑦ ⑧ ⑨ ⑩
FORGETFUL / CONFUSIONED	① ② ③ ④ ⑤ ⑥ ⑦ ⑧ ⑨ ⑩

HYPERACTIVITY

CONSTANTLY MOVING / TALKING	① ② ③ ④ ⑤ ⑥ ⑦ ⑧ ⑨ ⑩
STRUGGLING TO SIT STILL	① ② ③ ④ ⑤ ⑥ ⑦ ⑧ ⑨ ⑩
TOUCHING THINGS REPEATEDLY	① ② ③ ④ ⑤ ⑥ ⑦ ⑧ ⑨ ⑩
DIFFICULT SLEEPING	① ② ③ ④ ⑤ ⑥ ⑦ ⑧ ⑨ ⑩

IMPULSIVITY

ACTING WITHOUT THINKING	① ② ③ ④ ⑤ ⑥ ⑦ ⑧ ⑨ ⑩
INTERRUPTING OTHERS	① ② ③ ④ ⑤ ⑥ ⑦ ⑧ ⑨ ⑩
EASILY FRUSTRATED	① ② ③ ④ ⑤ ⑥ ⑦ ⑧ ⑨ ⑩
UNABLE TO HOLD BACKE MOTIONS	① ② ③ ④ ⑤ ⑥ ⑦ ⑧ ⑨ ⑩

MEALS

MEDICATIONS

WATER TRACKER

NOTES

....
....

<table>
<tr><td>

DAY GOALS

1 ....
2 ....
3 ....

</td><td>

DATE

WEEK

LOCATION

WEIGHT

</td></tr>
</table>

MOOD TRACKER

BEHAVIOR

INATTENTION

SHORT ATTENTION	① ② ③ ④ ⑤ ⑥ ⑦ ⑧ ⑨ ⑩
UNMOTIVATED / BORED	① ② ③ ④ ⑤ ⑥ ⑦ ⑧ ⑨ ⑩
SHORT ATTENTION	① ② ③ ④ ⑤ ⑥ ⑦ ⑧ ⑨ ⑩
FORGETFUL / CONFUSIONED	① ② ③ ④ ⑤ ⑥ ⑦ ⑧ ⑨ ⑩

HYPERACTIVITY

CONSTANTLY MOVING / TALKING	① ② ③ ④ ⑤ ⑥ ⑦ ⑧ ⑨ ⑩
STRUGGLING TO SIT STILL	① ② ③ ④ ⑤ ⑥ ⑦ ⑧ ⑨ ⑩
TOUCHING THINGS REPEATEDLY	① ② ③ ④ ⑤ ⑥ ⑦ ⑧ ⑨ ⑩
DIFFICULT SLEEPING	① ② ③ ④ ⑤ ⑥ ⑦ ⑧ ⑨ ⑩

IMPULSIVITY

ACTING WITHOUT THINKING	① ② ③ ④ ⑤ ⑥ ⑦ ⑧ ⑨ ⑩
INTERRUPTING OTHERS	① ② ③ ④ ⑤ ⑥ ⑦ ⑧ ⑨ ⑩
EASILY FRUSTRATED	① ② ③ ④ ⑤ ⑥ ⑦ ⑧ ⑨ ⑩
UNABLE TO HOLD BACKE MOTIONS	① ② ③ ④ ⑤ ⑥ ⑦ ⑧ ⑨ ⑩

MEALS	MEDICATIONS

WATER TRACKER

NOTES

....
....

1 ....

2 ....

3 ....

DATE

WEEK

LOCATION

WEIGHT

MOOD TRACKER

BEHAVIOR

INATTENTION

SHORT ATTENTION	① ② ③ ④ ⑤ ⑥ ⑦ ⑧ ⑨ ⑩
UNMOTIVATED / BORED	① ② ③ ④ ⑤ ⑥ ⑦ ⑧ ⑨ ⑩
SHORT ATTENTION	① ② ③ ④ ⑤ ⑥ ⑦ ⑧ ⑨ ⑩
FORGETFUL / CONFUSIONED	① ② ③ ④ ⑤ ⑥ ⑦ ⑧ ⑨ ⑩

HYPERACTIVITY

CONSTANTLY MOVING / TALKING	① ② ③ ④ ⑤ ⑥ ⑦ ⑧ ⑨ ⑩
STRUGGLING TO SIT STILL	① ② ③ ④ ⑤ ⑥ ⑦ ⑧ ⑨ ⑩
TOUCHING THINGS REPEATEDLY	① ② ③ ④ ⑤ ⑥ ⑦ ⑧ ⑨ ⑩
DIFFICULT SLEEPING	① ② ③ ④ ⑤ ⑥ ⑦ ⑧ ⑨ ⑩

IMPULSIVITY

ACTING WITHOUT THINKING	① ② ③ ④ ⑤ ⑥ ⑦ ⑧ ⑨ ⑩
INTERRUPTING OTHERS	① ② ③ ④ ⑤ ⑥ ⑦ ⑧ ⑨ ⑩
EASILY FRUSTRATED	① ② ③ ④ ⑤ ⑥ ⑦ ⑧ ⑨ ⑩
UNABLE TO HOLD BACKE MOTIONS	① ② ③ ④ ⑤ ⑥ ⑦ ⑧ ⑨ ⑩

MEALS

MEDICATIONS

WATER TRACKER

NOTES

....

....

DAY GOALS

1 ....
2 ....
3 ....

DATE
WEEK
LOCATION
WEIGHT

MOOD TRACKER

BEHAVIOR

INATTENTION

SHORT ATTENTION	① ② ③ ④ ⑤ ⑥ ⑦ ⑧ ⑨ ⑩
UNMOTIVATED / BORED	① ② ③ ④ ⑤ ⑥ ⑦ ⑧ ⑨ ⑩
SHORT ATTENTION	① ② ③ ④ ⑤ ⑥ ⑦ ⑧ ⑨ ⑩
FORGETFUL / CONFUSIONED	① ② ③ ④ ⑤ ⑥ ⑦ ⑧ ⑨ ⑩

HYPERACTIVITY

CONSTANTLY MOVING / TALKING	① ② ③ ④ ⑤ ⑥ ⑦ ⑧ ⑨ ⑩
STRUGGLING TO SIT STILL	① ② ③ ④ ⑤ ⑥ ⑦ ⑧ ⑨ ⑩
TOUCHING THINGS REPEATEDLY	① ② ③ ④ ⑤ ⑥ ⑦ ⑧ ⑨ ⑩
DIFFICULT SLEEPING	① ② ③ ④ ⑤ ⑥ ⑦ ⑧ ⑨ ⑩

IMPULSIVITY

ACTING WITHOUT THINKING	① ② ③ ④ ⑤ ⑥ ⑦ ⑧ ⑨ ⑩
INTERRUPTING OTHERS	① ② ③ ④ ⑤ ⑥ ⑦ ⑧ ⑨ ⑩
EASILY FRUSTRATED	① ② ③ ④ ⑤ ⑥ ⑦ ⑧ ⑨ ⑩
UNABLE TO HOLD BACKE MOTIONS	① ② ③ ④ ⑤ ⑥ ⑦ ⑧ ⑨ ⑩

MEALS

MEDICATIONS

WATER TRACKER

NOTES

....
....

DAY GOALS

1 ....
2 ....
3 ....

DATE
WEEK
LOCATION
WEIGHT

MOOD TRACKER

BEHAVIOR

INATTENTION

SHORT ATTENTION	① ② ③ ④ ⑤ ⑥ ⑦ ⑧ ⑨ ⑩
UNMOTIVATED / BORED	① ② ③ ④ ⑤ ⑥ ⑦ ⑧ ⑨ ⑩
SHORT ATTENTION	① ② ③ ④ ⑤ ⑥ ⑦ ⑧ ⑨ ⑩
FORGETFUL / CONFUSIONED	① ② ③ ④ ⑤ ⑥ ⑦ ⑧ ⑨ ⑩

HYPERACTIVITY

CONSTANTLY MOVING / TALKING	① ② ③ ④ ⑤ ⑥ ⑦ ⑧ ⑨ ⑩
STRUGGLING TO SIT STILL	① ② ③ ④ ⑤ ⑥ ⑦ ⑧ ⑨ ⑩
TOUCHING THINGS REPEATEDLY	① ② ③ ④ ⑤ ⑥ ⑦ ⑧ ⑨ ⑩
DIFFICULT SLEEPING	① ② ③ ④ ⑤ ⑥ ⑦ ⑧ ⑨ ⑩

IMPULSIVITY

ACTING WITHOUT THINKING	① ② ③ ④ ⑤ ⑥ ⑦ ⑧ ⑨ ⑩
INTERRUPTING OTHERS	① ② ③ ④ ⑤ ⑥ ⑦ ⑧ ⑨ ⑩
EASILY FRUSTRATED	① ② ③ ④ ⑤ ⑥ ⑦ ⑧ ⑨ ⑩
UNABLE TO HOLD BACKE MOTIONS	① ② ③ ④ ⑤ ⑥ ⑦ ⑧ ⑨ ⑩

MEALS

MEDICATIONS

WATER TRACKER

NOTES

....
....

DAY GOALS

1 ....
2 ....
3 ....

DATE
WEEK
LOCATION
WEIGHT

MOOD TRACKER

$\cdot\cdot$ $\cdot\cdot$ $><$ $\cdot\cdot$ $><$ $\smile$

BEHAVIOR

INATTENTION

SHORT ATTENTION	① ② ③ ④ ⑤ ⑥ ⑦ ⑧ ⑨ ⑩
UNMOTIVATED / BORED	① ② ③ ④ ⑤ ⑥ ⑦ ⑧ ⑨ ⑩
SHORT ATTENTION	① ② ③ ④ ⑤ ⑥ ⑦ ⑧ ⑨ ⑩
FORGETFUL / CONFUSIONED	① ② ③ ④ ⑤ ⑥ ⑦ ⑧ ⑨ ⑩

HYPERACTIVITY

CONSTANTLY MOVING / TALKING	① ② ③ ④ ⑤ ⑥ ⑦ ⑧ ⑨ ⑩
STRUGGLING TO SIT STILL	① ② ③ ④ ⑤ ⑥ ⑦ ⑧ ⑨ ⑩
TOUCHING THINGS REPEATEDLY	① ② ③ ④ ⑤ ⑥ ⑦ ⑧ ⑨ ⑩
DIFFICULT SLEEPING	① ② ③ ④ ⑤ ⑥ ⑦ ⑧ ⑨ ⑩

IMPULSIVITY

ACTING WITHOUT THINKING	① ② ③ ④ ⑤ ⑥ ⑦ ⑧ ⑨ ⑩
INTERRUPTING OTHERS	① ② ③ ④ ⑤ ⑥ ⑦ ⑧ ⑨ ⑩
EASILY FRUSTRATED	① ② ③ ④ ⑤ ⑥ ⑦ ⑧ ⑨ ⑩
UNABLE TO HOLD BACKE MOTIONS	① ② ③ ④ ⑤ ⑥ ⑦ ⑧ ⑨ ⑩

MEALS

MEDICATIONS

WATER TRACKER

NOTES

....
....

DAY GOALS

1 ....
2 ....
3 ....

DATE

WEEK

LOCATION

WEIGHT

MOOD TRACKER

😕 😐 😣 😢 😠 😁

BEHAVIOR

INATTENTION

SHORT ATTENTION	① ② ③ ④ ⑤ ⑥ ⑦ ⑧ ⑨ ⑩
UNMOTIVATED / BORED	① ② ③ ④ ⑤ ⑥ ⑦ ⑧ ⑨ ⑩
SHORT ATTENTION	① ② ③ ④ ⑤ ⑥ ⑦ ⑧ ⑨ ⑩
FORGETFUL / CONFUSIONED	① ② ③ ④ ⑤ ⑥ ⑦ ⑧ ⑨ ⑩

HYPERACTIVITY

CONSTANTLY MOVING / TALKING	① ② ③ ④ ⑤ ⑥ ⑦ ⑧ ⑨ ⑩
STRUGGLING TO SIT STILL	① ② ③ ④ ⑤ ⑥ ⑦ ⑧ ⑨ ⑩
TOUCHING THINGS REPEATEDLY	① ② ③ ④ ⑤ ⑥ ⑦ ⑧ ⑨ ⑩
DIFFICULT SLEEPING	① ② ③ ④ ⑤ ⑥ ⑦ ⑧ ⑨ ⑩

IMPULSIVITY

ACTING WITHOUT THINKING	① ② ③ ④ ⑤ ⑥ ⑦ ⑧ ⑨ ⑩
INTERRUPTING OTHERS	① ② ③ ④ ⑤ ⑥ ⑦ ⑧ ⑨ ⑩
EASILY FRUSTRATED	① ② ③ ④ ⑤ ⑥ ⑦ ⑧ ⑨ ⑩
UNABLE TO HOLD BACKE MOTIONS	① ② ③ ④ ⑤ ⑥ ⑦ ⑧ ⑨ ⑩

MEALS

MEDICATIONS

WATER TRACKER

NOTES

....
....

DAY GOALS

1 ....
2 ....
3 ....

DATE

WEEK

LOCATION

WEIGHT

MOOD TRACKER

BEHAVIOR

INATTENTION

SHORT ATTENTION	① ② ③ ④ ⑤ ⑥ ⑦ ⑧ ⑨ ⑩
UNMOTIVATED / BORED	① ② ③ ④ ⑤ ⑥ ⑦ ⑧ ⑨ ⑩
SHORT ATTENTION	① ② ③ ④ ⑤ ⑥ ⑦ ⑧ ⑨ ⑩
FORGETFUL / CONFUSIONED	① ② ③ ④ ⑤ ⑥ ⑦ ⑧ ⑨ ⑩

HYPERACTIVITY

CONSTANTLY MOVING / TALKING	① ② ③ ④ ⑤ ⑥ ⑦ ⑧ ⑨ ⑩
STRUGGLING TO SIT STILL	① ② ③ ④ ⑤ ⑥ ⑦ ⑧ ⑨ ⑩
TOUCHING THINGS REPEATEDLY	① ② ③ ④ ⑤ ⑥ ⑦ ⑧ ⑨ ⑩
DIFFICULT SLEEPING	① ② ③ ④ ⑤ ⑥ ⑦ ⑧ ⑨ ⑩

IMPULSIVITY

ACTING WITHOUT THINKING	① ② ③ ④ ⑤ ⑥ ⑦ ⑧ ⑨ ⑩
INTERRUPTING OTHERS	① ② ③ ④ ⑤ ⑥ ⑦ ⑧ ⑨ ⑩
EASILY FRUSTRATED	① ② ③ ④ ⑤ ⑥ ⑦ ⑧ ⑨ ⑩
UNABLE TO HOLD BACKE MOTIONS	① ② ③ ④ ⑤ ⑥ ⑦ ⑧ ⑨ ⑩

MEALS

MEDICATIONS

WATER TRACKER

NOTES

....
....

MOOD TRACKER   🙁 😐 😖 😢 😠 😃

BEHAVIOR

INATTENTION

SHORT ATTENTION	① ② ③ ④ ⑤ ⑥ ⑦ ⑧ ⑨ ⑩
UNMOTIVATED / BORED	① ② ③ ④ ⑤ ⑥ ⑦ ⑧ ⑨ ⑩
SHORT ATTENTION	① ② ③ ④ ⑤ ⑥ ⑦ ⑧ ⑨ ⑩
FORGETFUL / CONFUSIONED	① ② ③ ④ ⑤ ⑥ ⑦ ⑧ ⑨ ⑩

HYPERACTIVITY

CONSTANTLY MOVING / TALKING	① ② ③ ④ ⑤ ⑥ ⑦ ⑧ ⑨ ⑩
STRUGGLING TO SIT STILL	① ② ③ ④ ⑤ ⑥ ⑦ ⑧ ⑨ ⑩
TOUCHING THINGS REPEATEDLY	① ② ③ ④ ⑤ ⑥ ⑦ ⑧ ⑨ ⑩
DIFFICULT SLEEPING	① ② ③ ④ ⑤ ⑥ ⑦ ⑧ ⑨ ⑩

IMPULSIVITY

ACTING WITHOUT THINKING	① ② ③ ④ ⑤ ⑥ ⑦ ⑧ ⑨ ⑩
INTERRUPTING OTHERS	① ② ③ ④ ⑤ ⑥ ⑦ ⑧ ⑨ ⑩
EASILY FRUSTRATED	① ② ③ ④ ⑤ ⑥ ⑦ ⑧ ⑨ ⑩
UNABLE TO HOLD BACKE MOTIONS	① ② ③ ④ ⑤ ⑥ ⑦ ⑧ ⑨ ⑩

MEALS

MEDICATIONS

WATER TRACKER   ⬚ ⬚ ⬚ ⬚ ⬚ ⬚ ⬚

NOTES

....
....

DAY GOALS

1 ....
2 ....
3 ....

DATE
WEEK
LOCATION
WEIGHT

MOOD TRACKER

BEHAVIOR

INATTENTION

SHORT ATTENTION	① ② ③ ④ ⑤ ⑥ ⑦ ⑧ ⑨ ⑩
UNMOTIVATED / BORED	① ② ③ ④ ⑤ ⑥ ⑦ ⑧ ⑨ ⑩
SHORT ATTENTION	① ② ③ ④ ⑤ ⑥ ⑦ ⑧ ⑨ ⑩
FORGETFUL / CONFUSIONED	① ② ③ ④ ⑤ ⑥ ⑦ ⑧ ⑨ ⑩

HYPERACTIVITY

CONSTANTLY MOVING / TALKING	① ② ③ ④ ⑤ ⑥ ⑦ ⑧ ⑨ ⑩
STRUGGLING TO SIT STILL	① ② ③ ④ ⑤ ⑥ ⑦ ⑧ ⑨ ⑩
TOUCHING THINGS REPEATEDLY	① ② ③ ④ ⑤ ⑥ ⑦ ⑧ ⑨ ⑩
DIFFICULT SLEEPING	① ② ③ ④ ⑤ ⑥ ⑦ ⑧ ⑨ ⑩

IMPULSIVITY

ACTING WITHOUT THINKING	① ② ③ ④ ⑤ ⑥ ⑦ ⑧ ⑨ ⑩
INTERRUPTING OTHERS	① ② ③ ④ ⑤ ⑥ ⑦ ⑧ ⑨ ⑩
EASILY FRUSTRATED	① ② ③ ④ ⑤ ⑥ ⑦ ⑧ ⑨ ⑩
UNABLE TO HOLD BACKE MOTIONS	① ② ③ ④ ⑤ ⑥ ⑦ ⑧ ⑨ ⑩

MEALS

MEDICATIONS

WATER TRACKER

NOTES

....
....

1 ....
2 ....
3 ....

DATE
WEEK
LOCATION
WEIGHT

MOOD TRACKER

BEHAVIOR

INATTENTION

SHORT ATTENTION	① ② ③ ④ ⑤ ⑥ ⑦ ⑧ ⑨ ⑩
UNMOTIVATED / BORED	① ② ③ ④ ⑤ ⑥ ⑦ ⑧ ⑨ ⑩
SHORT ATTENTION	① ② ③ ④ ⑤ ⑥ ⑦ ⑧ ⑨ ⑩
FORGETFUL / CONFUSIONED	① ② ③ ④ ⑤ ⑥ ⑦ ⑧ ⑨ ⑩

HYPERACTIVITY

CONSTANTLY MOVING / TALKING	① ② ③ ④ ⑤ ⑥ ⑦ ⑧ ⑨ ⑩
STRUGGLING TO SIT STILL	① ② ③ ④ ⑤ ⑥ ⑦ ⑧ ⑨ ⑩
TOUCHING THINGS REPEATEDLY	① ② ③ ④ ⑤ ⑥ ⑦ ⑧ ⑨ ⑩
DIFFICULT SLEEPING	① ② ③ ④ ⑤ ⑥ ⑦ ⑧ ⑨ ⑩

IMPULSIVITY

ACTING WITHOUT THINKING	① ② ③ ④ ⑤ ⑥ ⑦ ⑧ ⑨ ⑩
INTERRUPTING OTHERS	① ② ③ ④ ⑤ ⑥ ⑦ ⑧ ⑨ ⑩
EASILY FRUSTRATED	① ② ③ ④ ⑤ ⑥ ⑦ ⑧ ⑨ ⑩
UNABLE TO HOLD BACKE MOTIONS	① ② ③ ④ ⑤ ⑥ ⑦ ⑧ ⑨ ⑩

MEALS

MEDICATIONS

WATER TRACKER

NOTES

....
....

DAY GOALS

1 ....
2 ....
3 ....

DATE
WEEK
LOCATION
WEIGHT

MOOD TRACKER

BEHAVIOR

INATTENTION

SHORT ATTENTION	① ② ③ ④ ⑤ ⑥ ⑦ ⑧ ⑨ ⑩
UNMOTIVATED / BORED	① ② ③ ④ ⑤ ⑥ ⑦ ⑧ ⑨ ⑩
SHORT ATTENTION	① ② ③ ④ ⑤ ⑥ ⑦ ⑧ ⑨ ⑩
FORGETFUL / CONFUSIONED	① ② ③ ④ ⑤ ⑥ ⑦ ⑧ ⑨ ⑩

HYPERACTIVITY

CONSTANTLY MOVING / TALKING	① ② ③ ④ ⑤ ⑥ ⑦ ⑧ ⑨ ⑩
STRUGGLING TO SIT STILL	① ② ③ ④ ⑤ ⑥ ⑦ ⑧ ⑨ ⑩
TOUCHING THINGS REPEATEDLY	① ② ③ ④ ⑤ ⑥ ⑦ ⑧ ⑨ ⑩
DIFFICULT SLEEPING	① ② ③ ④ ⑤ ⑥ ⑦ ⑧ ⑨ ⑩

IMPULSIVITY

ACTING WITHOUT THINKING	① ② ③ ④ ⑤ ⑥ ⑦ ⑧ ⑨ ⑩
INTERRUPTING OTHERS	① ② ③ ④ ⑤ ⑥ ⑦ ⑧ ⑨ ⑩
EASILY FRUSTRATED	① ② ③ ④ ⑤ ⑥ ⑦ ⑧ ⑨ ⑩
UNABLE TO HOLD BACKE MOTIONS	① ② ③ ④ ⑤ ⑥ ⑦ ⑧ ⑨ ⑩

MEALS

MEDICATIONS

WATER TRACKER

NOTES

....
....

DAY GOALS

1 ....
2 ....
3 ....

DATE

WEEK

LOCATION

WEIGHT

MOOD TRACKER

BEHAVIOR

INATTENTION

SHORT ATTENTION	① ② ③ ④ ⑤ ⑥ ⑦ ⑧ ⑨ ⑩
UNMOTIVATED / BORED	① ② ③ ④ ⑤ ⑥ ⑦ ⑧ ⑨ ⑩
SHORT ATTENTION	① ② ③ ④ ⑤ ⑥ ⑦ ⑧ ⑨ ⑩
FORGETFUL / CONFUSIONED	① ② ③ ④ ⑤ ⑥ ⑦ ⑧ ⑨ ⑩

HYPERACTIVITY

CONSTANTLY MOVING / TALKING	① ② ③ ④ ⑤ ⑥ ⑦ ⑧ ⑨ ⑩
STRUGGLING TO SIT STILL	① ② ③ ④ ⑤ ⑥ ⑦ ⑧ ⑨ ⑩
TOUCHING THINGS REPEATEDLY	① ② ③ ④ ⑤ ⑥ ⑦ ⑧ ⑨ ⑩
DIFFICULT SLEEPING	① ② ③ ④ ⑤ ⑥ ⑦ ⑧ ⑨ ⑩

IMPULSIVITY

ACTING WITHOUT THINKING	① ② ③ ④ ⑤ ⑥ ⑦ ⑧ ⑨ ⑩
INTERRUPTING OTHERS	① ② ③ ④ ⑤ ⑥ ⑦ ⑧ ⑨ ⑩
EASILY FRUSTRATED	① ② ③ ④ ⑤ ⑥ ⑦ ⑧ ⑨ ⑩
UNABLE TO HOLD BACKE MOTIONS	① ② ③ ④ ⑤ ⑥ ⑦ ⑧ ⑨ ⑩

MEALS

MEDICATIONS

WATER TRACKER

NOTES

....
....

DAY GOALS

1 ....
2 ....
3 ....

DATE
WEEK
LOCATION
WEIGHT

MOOD TRACKER

BEHAVIOR

INATTENTION

SHORT ATTENTION	① ② ③ ④ ⑤ ⑥ ⑦ ⑧ ⑨ ⑩
UNMOTIVATED / BORED	① ② ③ ④ ⑤ ⑥ ⑦ ⑧ ⑨ ⑩
SHORT ATTENTION	① ② ③ ④ ⑤ ⑥ ⑦ ⑧ ⑨ ⑩
FORGETFUL / CONFUSIONED	① ② ③ ④ ⑤ ⑥ ⑦ ⑧ ⑨ ⑩

HYPERACTIVITY

CONSTANTLY MOVING / TALKING	① ② ③ ④ ⑤ ⑥ ⑦ ⑧ ⑨ ⑩
STRUGGLING TO SIT STILL	① ② ③ ④ ⑤ ⑥ ⑦ ⑧ ⑨ ⑩
TOUCHING THINGS REPEATEDLY	① ② ③ ④ ⑤ ⑥ ⑦ ⑧ ⑨ ⑩
DIFFICULT SLEEPING	① ② ③ ④ ⑤ ⑥ ⑦ ⑧ ⑨ ⑩

IMPULSIVITY

ACTING WITHOUT THINKING	① ② ③ ④ ⑤ ⑥ ⑦ ⑧ ⑨ ⑩
INTERRUPTING OTHERS	① ② ③ ④ ⑤ ⑥ ⑦ ⑧ ⑨ ⑩
EASILY FRUSTRATED	① ② ③ ④ ⑤ ⑥ ⑦ ⑧ ⑨ ⑩
UNABLE TO HOLD BACKE MOTIONS	① ② ③ ④ ⑤ ⑥ ⑦ ⑧ ⑨ ⑩

MEALS

MEDICATIONS

WATER TRACKER

NOTES

....
....

DAY GOALS

1 ....
2 ....
3 ....

DATE

WEEK

LOCATION

WEIGHT

MOOD TRACKER

BEHAVIOR

INATTENTION

SHORT ATTENTION	① ② ③ ④ ⑤ ⑥ ⑦ ⑧ ⑨ ⑩
UNMOTIVATED / BORED	① ② ③ ④ ⑤ ⑥ ⑦ ⑧ ⑨ ⑩
SHORT ATTENTION	① ② ③ ④ ⑤ ⑥ ⑦ ⑧ ⑨ ⑩
FORGETFUL / CONFUSIONED	① ② ③ ④ ⑤ ⑥ ⑦ ⑧ ⑨ ⑩

HYPERACTIVITY

CONSTANTLY MOVING / TALKING	① ② ③ ④ ⑤ ⑥ ⑦ ⑧ ⑨ ⑩
STRUGGLING TO SIT STILL	① ② ③ ④ ⑤ ⑥ ⑦ ⑧ ⑨ ⑩
TOUCHING THINGS REPEATEDLY	① ② ③ ④ ⑤ ⑥ ⑦ ⑧ ⑨ ⑩
DIFFICULT SLEEPING	① ② ③ ④ ⑤ ⑥ ⑦ ⑧ ⑨ ⑩

IMPULSIVITY

ACTING WITHOUT THINKING	① ② ③ ④ ⑤ ⑥ ⑦ ⑧ ⑨ ⑩
INTERRUPTING OTHERS	① ② ③ ④ ⑤ ⑥ ⑦ ⑧ ⑨ ⑩
EASILY FRUSTRATED	① ② ③ ④ ⑤ ⑥ ⑦ ⑧ ⑨ ⑩
UNABLE TO HOLD BACKE MOTIONS	① ② ③ ④ ⑤ ⑥ ⑦ ⑧ ⑨ ⑩

MEALS

MEDICATIONS

WATER TRACKER

NOTES

....
....

DAY GOALS

1 ....
2 ....
3 ....

DATE
WEEK
LOCATION
WEIGHT

MOOD TRACKER

BEHAVIOR

INATTENTION

SHORT ATTENTION	① ② ③ ④ ⑤ ⑥ ⑦ ⑧ ⑨ ⑩
UNMOTIVATED / BORED	① ② ③ ④ ⑤ ⑥ ⑦ ⑧ ⑨ ⑩
SHORT ATTENTION	① ② ③ ④ ⑤ ⑥ ⑦ ⑧ ⑨ ⑩
FORGETFUL / CONFUSIONED	① ② ③ ④ ⑤ ⑥ ⑦ ⑧ ⑨ ⑩

HYPERACTIVITY

CONSTANTLY MOVING / TALKING	① ② ③ ④ ⑤ ⑥ ⑦ ⑧ ⑨ ⑩
STRUGGLING TO SIT STILL	① ② ③ ④ ⑤ ⑥ ⑦ ⑧ ⑨ ⑩
TOUCHING THINGS REPEATEDLY	① ② ③ ④ ⑤ ⑥ ⑦ ⑧ ⑨ ⑩
DIFFICULT SLEEPING	① ② ③ ④ ⑤ ⑥ ⑦ ⑧ ⑨ ⑩

IMPULSIVITY

ACTING WITHOUT THINKING	① ② ③ ④ ⑤ ⑥ ⑦ ⑧ ⑨ ⑩
INTERRUPTING OTHERS	① ② ③ ④ ⑤ ⑥ ⑦ ⑧ ⑨ ⑩
EASILY FRUSTRATED	① ② ③ ④ ⑤ ⑥ ⑦ ⑧ ⑨ ⑩
UNABLE TO HOLD BACKE MOTIONS	① ② ③ ④ ⑤ ⑥ ⑦ ⑧ ⑨ ⑩

MEALS

MEDICATIONS

WATER TRACKER

NOTES

....
....

DAY GOALS

1 ....
2 ....
3 ....

DATE

WEEK

LOCATION

WEIGHT

MOOD TRACKER

BEHAVIOR

INATTENTION

SHORT ATTENTION	①②③④⑤⑥⑦⑧⑨⑩
UNMOTIVATED / BORED	①②③④⑤⑥⑦⑧⑨⑩
SHORT ATTENTION	①②③④⑤⑥⑦⑧⑨⑩
FORGETFUL / CONFUSIONED	①②③④⑤⑥⑦⑧⑨⑩

HYPERACTIVITY

CONSTANTLY MOVING / TALKING	①②③④⑤⑥⑦⑧⑨⑩
STRUGGLING TO SIT STILL	①②③④⑤⑥⑦⑧⑨⑩
TOUCHING THINGS REPEATEDLY	①②③④⑤⑥⑦⑧⑨⑩
DIFFICULT SLEEPING	①②③④⑤⑥⑦⑧⑨⑩

IMPULSIVITY

ACTING WITHOUT THINKING	①②③④⑤⑥⑦⑧⑨⑩
INTERRUPTING OTHERS	①②③④⑤⑥⑦⑧⑨⑩
EASILY FRUSTRATED	①②③④⑤⑥⑦⑧⑨⑩
UNABLE TO HOLD BACKE MOTIONS	①②③④⑤⑥⑦⑧⑨⑩

MEALS

MEDICATIONS

WATER TRACKER

NOTES

....
....

DAY GOALS

1 ....
2 ....
3 ....

DATE
WEEK
LOCATION
WEIGHT

MOOD TRACKER

BEHAVIOR

INATTENTION

SHORT ATTENTION	① ② ③ ④ ⑤ ⑥ ⑦ ⑧ ⑨ ⑩
UNMOTIVATED / BORED	① ② ③ ④ ⑤ ⑥ ⑦ ⑧ ⑨ ⑩
SHORT ATTENTION	① ② ③ ④ ⑤ ⑥ ⑦ ⑧ ⑨ ⑩
FORGETFUL / CONFUSIONED	① ② ③ ④ ⑤ ⑥ ⑦ ⑧ ⑨ ⑩

HYPERACTIVITY

CONSTANTLY MOVING / TALKING	① ② ③ ④ ⑤ ⑥ ⑦ ⑧ ⑨ ⑩
STRUGGLING TO SIT STILL	① ② ③ ④ ⑤ ⑥ ⑦ ⑧ ⑨ ⑩
TOUCHING THINGS REPEATEDLY	① ② ③ ④ ⑤ ⑥ ⑦ ⑧ ⑨ ⑩
DIFFICULT SLEEPING	① ② ③ ④ ⑤ ⑥ ⑦ ⑧ ⑨ ⑩

IMPULSIVITY

ACTING WITHOUT THINKING	① ② ③ ④ ⑤ ⑥ ⑦ ⑧ ⑨ ⑩
INTERRUPTING OTHERS	① ② ③ ④ ⑤ ⑥ ⑦ ⑧ ⑨ ⑩
EASILY FRUSTRATED	① ② ③ ④ ⑤ ⑥ ⑦ ⑧ ⑨ ⑩
UNABLE TO HOLD BACKE MOTIONS	① ② ③ ④ ⑤ ⑥ ⑦ ⑧ ⑨ ⑩

MEALS

MEDICATIONS

WATER TRACKER

NOTES

....
....

DAY GOALS

1 ....
2 ....
3 ....

DATE

WEEK

LOCATION

WEIGHT

MOOD TRACKER

BEHAVIOR

INATTENTION

SHORT ATTENTION	① ② ③ ④ ⑤ ⑥ ⑦ ⑧ ⑨ ⑩
UNMOTIVATED / BORED	① ② ③ ④ ⑤ ⑥ ⑦ ⑧ ⑨ ⑩
SHORT ATTENTION	① ② ③ ④ ⑤ ⑥ ⑦ ⑧ ⑨ ⑩
FORGETFUL / CONFUSIONED	① ② ③ ④ ⑤ ⑥ ⑦ ⑧ ⑨ ⑩

HYPERACTIVITY

CONSTANTLY MOVING / TALKING	① ② ③ ④ ⑤ ⑥ ⑦ ⑧ ⑨ ⑩
STRUGGLING TO SIT STILL	① ② ③ ④ ⑤ ⑥ ⑦ ⑧ ⑨ ⑩
TOUCHING THINGS REPEATEDLY	① ② ③ ④ ⑤ ⑥ ⑦ ⑧ ⑨ ⑩
DIFFICULT SLEEPING	① ② ③ ④ ⑤ ⑥ ⑦ ⑧ ⑨ ⑩

IMPULSIVITY

ACTING WITHOUT THINKING	① ② ③ ④ ⑤ ⑥ ⑦ ⑧ ⑨ ⑩
INTERRUPTING OTHERS	① ② ③ ④ ⑤ ⑥ ⑦ ⑧ ⑨ ⑩
EASILY FRUSTRATED	① ② ③ ④ ⑤ ⑥ ⑦ ⑧ ⑨ ⑩
UNABLE TO HOLD BACKE MOTIONS	① ② ③ ④ ⑤ ⑥ ⑦ ⑧ ⑨ ⑩

MEALS

MEDICATIONS

WATER TRACKER

NOTES

....
....

DAY GOALS

1 ....
2 ....
3 ....

DATE

WEEK

LOCATION

WEIGHT

MOOD TRACKER

BEHAVIOR

INATTENTION

SHORT ATTENTION	(1)(2)(3)(4)(5)(6)(7)(8)(9)(10)
UNMOTIVATED / BORED	(1)(2)(3)(4)(5)(6)(7)(8)(9)(10)
SHORT ATTENTION	(1)(2)(3)(4)(5)(6)(7)(8)(9)(10)
FORGETFUL / CONFUSIONED	(1)(2)(3)(4)(5)(6)(7)(8)(9)(10)

HYPERACTIVITY

CONSTANTLY MOVING / TALKING	(1)(2)(3)(4)(5)(6)(7)(8)(9)(10)
STRUGGLING TO SIT STILL	(1)(2)(3)(4)(5)(6)(7)(8)(9)(10)
TOUCHING THINGS REPEATEDLY	(1)(2)(3)(4)(5)(6)(7)(8)(9)(10)
DIFFICULT SLEEPING	(1)(2)(3)(4)(5)(6)(7)(8)(9)(10)

IMPULSIVITY

ACTING WITHOUT THINKING	(1)(2)(3)(4)(5)(6)(7)(8)(9)(10)
INTERRUPTING OTHERS	(1)(2)(3)(4)(5)(6)(7)(8)(9)(10)
EASILY FRUSTRATED	(1)(2)(3)(4)(5)(6)(7)(8)(9)(10)
UNABLE TO HOLD BACKE MOTIONS	(1)(2)(3)(4)(5)(6)(7)(8)(9)(10)

MEALS

MEDICATIONS

WATER TRACKER

NOTES

....
....

DAY GOALS

1 ....
2 ....
3 ....

DATE

WEEK

LOCATION

WEIGHT

MOOD TRACKER

BEHAVIOR

INATTENTION

SHORT ATTENTION	① ② ③ ④ ⑤ ⑥ ⑦ ⑧ ⑨ ⑩
UNMOTIVATED / BORED	① ② ③ ④ ⑤ ⑥ ⑦ ⑧ ⑨ ⑩
SHORT ATTENTION	① ② ③ ④ ⑤ ⑥ ⑦ ⑧ ⑨ ⑩
FORGETFUL / CONFUSIONED	① ② ③ ④ ⑤ ⑥ ⑦ ⑧ ⑨ ⑩

HYPERACTIVITY

CONSTANTLY MOVING / TALKING	① ② ③ ④ ⑤ ⑥ ⑦ ⑧ ⑨ ⑩
STRUGGLING TO SIT STILL	① ② ③ ④ ⑤ ⑥ ⑦ ⑧ ⑨ ⑩
TOUCHING THINGS REPEATEDLY	① ② ③ ④ ⑤ ⑥ ⑦ ⑧ ⑨ ⑩
DIFFICULT SLEEPING	① ② ③ ④ ⑤ ⑥ ⑦ ⑧ ⑨ ⑩

IMPULSIVITY

ACTING WITHOUT THINKING	① ② ③ ④ ⑤ ⑥ ⑦ ⑧ ⑨ ⑩
INTERRUPTING OTHERS	① ② ③ ④ ⑤ ⑥ ⑦ ⑧ ⑨ ⑩
EASILY FRUSTRATED	① ② ③ ④ ⑤ ⑥ ⑦ ⑧ ⑨ ⑩
UNABLE TO HOLD BACKE MOTIONS	① ② ③ ④ ⑤ ⑥ ⑦ ⑧ ⑨ ⑩

MEALS

MEDICATIONS

WATER TRACKER

NOTES

....
....

DAY GOALS

1 ....
2 ....
3 ....

DATE
WEEK
LOCATION
WEIGHT

MOOD TRACKER

BEHAVIOR

INATTENTION

SHORT ATTENTION	① ② ③ ④ ⑤ ⑥ ⑦ ⑧ ⑨ ⑩
UNMOTIVATED / BORED	① ② ③ ④ ⑤ ⑥ ⑦ ⑧ ⑨ ⑩
SHORT ATTENTION	① ② ③ ④ ⑤ ⑥ ⑦ ⑧ ⑨ ⑩
FORGETFUL / CONFUSIONED	① ② ③ ④ ⑤ ⑥ ⑦ ⑧ ⑨ ⑩

HYPERACTIVITY

CONSTANTLY MOVING / TALKING	① ② ③ ④ ⑤ ⑥ ⑦ ⑧ ⑨ ⑩
STRUGGLING TO SIT STILL	① ② ③ ④ ⑤ ⑥ ⑦ ⑧ ⑨ ⑩
TOUCHING THINGS REPEATEDLY	① ② ③ ④ ⑤ ⑥ ⑦ ⑧ ⑨ ⑩
DIFFICULT SLEEPING	① ② ③ ④ ⑤ ⑥ ⑦ ⑧ ⑨ ⑩

IMPULSIVITY

ACTING WITHOUT THINKING	① ② ③ ④ ⑤ ⑥ ⑦ ⑧ ⑨ ⑩
INTERRUPTING OTHERS	① ② ③ ④ ⑤ ⑥ ⑦ ⑧ ⑨ ⑩
EASILY FRUSTRATED	① ② ③ ④ ⑤ ⑥ ⑦ ⑧ ⑨ ⑩
UNABLE TO HOLD BACKE MOTIONS	① ② ③ ④ ⑤ ⑥ ⑦ ⑧ ⑨ ⑩

MEALS

MEDICATIONS

WATER TRACKER

NOTES

....
....

DAY GOALS

1 ....
2 ....
3 ....

DATE

WEEK

LOCATION

WEIGHT

MOOD TRACKER

BEHAVIOR

INATTENTION

SHORT ATTENTION	① ② ③ ④ ⑤ ⑥ ⑦ ⑧ ⑨ ⑩
UNMOTIVATED / BORED	① ② ③ ④ ⑤ ⑥ ⑦ ⑧ ⑨ ⑩
SHORT ATTENTION	① ② ③ ④ ⑤ ⑥ ⑦ ⑧ ⑨ ⑩
FORGETFUL / CONFUSIONED	① ② ③ ④ ⑤ ⑥ ⑦ ⑧ ⑨ ⑩

HYPERACTIVITY

CONSTANTLY MOVING / TALKING	① ② ③ ④ ⑤ ⑥ ⑦ ⑧ ⑨ ⑩
STRUGGLING TO SIT STILL	① ② ③ ④ ⑤ ⑥ ⑦ ⑧ ⑨ ⑩
TOUCHING THINGS REPEATEDLY	① ② ③ ④ ⑤ ⑥ ⑦ ⑧ ⑨ ⑩
DIFFICULT SLEEPING	① ② ③ ④ ⑤ ⑥ ⑦ ⑧ ⑨ ⑩

IMPULSIVITY

ACTING WITHOUT THINKING	① ② ③ ④ ⑤ ⑥ ⑦ ⑧ ⑨ ⑩
INTERRUPTING OTHERS	① ② ③ ④ ⑤ ⑥ ⑦ ⑧ ⑨ ⑩
EASILY FRUSTRATED	① ② ③ ④ ⑤ ⑥ ⑦ ⑧ ⑨ ⑩
UNABLE TO HOLD BACKE MOTIONS	① ② ③ ④ ⑤ ⑥ ⑦ ⑧ ⑨ ⑩

MEALS

MEDICATIONS

WATER TRACKER

NOTES

....
....

DAY GOALS

1 ....
2 ....
3 ....

DATE
WEEK
LOCATION
WEIGHT

MOOD TRACKER

BEHAVIOR

INATTENTION

SHORT ATTENTION	① ② ③ ④ ⑤ ⑥ ⑦ ⑧ ⑨ ⑩
UNMOTIVATED / BORED	① ② ③ ④ ⑤ ⑥ ⑦ ⑧ ⑨ ⑩
SHORT ATTENTION	① ② ③ ④ ⑤ ⑥ ⑦ ⑧ ⑨ ⑩
FORGETFUL / CONFUSIONED	① ② ③ ④ ⑤ ⑥ ⑦ ⑧ ⑨ ⑩

HYPERACTIVITY

CONSTANTLY MOVING / TALKING	① ② ③ ④ ⑤ ⑥ ⑦ ⑧ ⑨ ⑩
STRUGGLING TO SIT STILL	① ② ③ ④ ⑤ ⑥ ⑦ ⑧ ⑨ ⑩
TOUCHING THINGS REPEATEDLY	① ② ③ ④ ⑤ ⑥ ⑦ ⑧ ⑨ ⑩
DIFFICULT SLEEPING	① ② ③ ④ ⑤ ⑥ ⑦ ⑧ ⑨ ⑩

IMPULSIVITY

ACTING WITHOUT THINKING	① ② ③ ④ ⑤ ⑥ ⑦ ⑧ ⑨ ⑩
INTERRUPTING OTHERS	① ② ③ ④ ⑤ ⑥ ⑦ ⑧ ⑨ ⑩
EASILY FRUSTRATED	① ② ③ ④ ⑤ ⑥ ⑦ ⑧ ⑨ ⑩
UNABLE TO HOLD BACKE MOTIONS	① ② ③ ④ ⑤ ⑥ ⑦ ⑧ ⑨ ⑩

MEALS

MEDICATIONS

WATER TRACKER

NOTES

....
....

DAY GOALS

1 ....
2 ....
3 ....

DATE
WEEK
LOCATION
WEIGHT

MOOD TRACKER

BEHAVIOR

INATTENTION

SHORT ATTENTION	①②③④⑤⑥⑦⑧⑨⑩
UNMOTIVATED / BORED	①②③④⑤⑥⑦⑧⑨⑩
SHORT ATTENTION	①②③④⑤⑥⑦⑧⑨⑩
FORGETFUL / CONFUSIONED	①②③④⑤⑥⑦⑧⑨⑩

HYPERACTIVITY

CONSTANTLY MOVING / TALKING	①②③④⑤⑥⑦⑧⑨⑩
STRUGGLING TO SIT STILL	①②③④⑤⑥⑦⑧⑨⑩
TOUCHING THINGS REPEATEDLY	①②③④⑤⑥⑦⑧⑨⑩
DIFFICULT SLEEPING	①②③④⑤⑥⑦⑧⑨⑩

IMPULSIVITY

ACTING WITHOUT THINKING	①②③④⑤⑥⑦⑧⑨⑩
INTERRUPTING OTHERS	①②③④⑤⑥⑦⑧⑨⑩
EASILY FRUSTRATED	①②③④⑤⑥⑦⑧⑨⑩
UNABLE TO HOLD BACKE MOTIONS	①②③④⑤⑥⑦⑧⑨⑩

MEALS

MEDICATIONS

WATER TRACKER

NOTES

....
....

DAY GOALS

1 ....
2 ....
3 ....

DATE
WEEK
LOCATION
WEIGHT

MOOD TRACKER

BEHAVIOR

INATTENTION

SHORT ATTENTION	① ② ③ ④ ⑤ ⑥ ⑦ ⑧ ⑨ ⑩
UNMOTIVATED / BORED	① ② ③ ④ ⑤ ⑥ ⑦ ⑧ ⑨ ⑩
SHORT ATTENTION	① ② ③ ④ ⑤ ⑥ ⑦ ⑧ ⑨ ⑩
FORGETFUL / CONFUSIONED	① ② ③ ④ ⑤ ⑥ ⑦ ⑧ ⑨ ⑩

HYPERACTIVITY

CONSTANTLY MOVING / TALKING	① ② ③ ④ ⑤ ⑥ ⑦ ⑧ ⑨ ⑩
STRUGGLING TO SIT STILL	① ② ③ ④ ⑤ ⑥ ⑦ ⑧ ⑨ ⑩
TOUCHING THINGS REPEATEDLY	① ② ③ ④ ⑤ ⑥ ⑦ ⑧ ⑨ ⑩
DIFFICULT SLEEPING	① ② ③ ④ ⑤ ⑥ ⑦ ⑧ ⑨ ⑩

IMPULSIVITY

ACTING WITHOUT THINKING	① ② ③ ④ ⑤ ⑥ ⑦ ⑧ ⑨ ⑩
INTERRUPTING OTHERS	① ② ③ ④ ⑤ ⑥ ⑦ ⑧ ⑨ ⑩
EASILY FRUSTRATED	① ② ③ ④ ⑤ ⑥ ⑦ ⑧ ⑨ ⑩
UNABLE TO HOLD BACKE MOTIONS	① ② ③ ④ ⑤ ⑥ ⑦ ⑧ ⑨ ⑩

MEALS

MEDICATIONS

WATER TRACKER

NOTES

....
....

DAY GOALS

1 ....

2 ....

3 ....

DATE

WEEK

LOCATION

WEIGHT

MOOD TRACKER

😕 😐 😣 😢 😠 😃

BEHAVIOR

INATTENTION

SHORT ATTENTION	① ② ③ ④ ⑤ ⑥ ⑦ ⑧ ⑨ ⑩
UNMOTIVATED / BORED	① ② ③ ④ ⑤ ⑥ ⑦ ⑧ ⑨ ⑩
SHORT ATTENTION	① ② ③ ④ ⑤ ⑥ ⑦ ⑧ ⑨ ⑩
FORGETFUL / CONFUSIONED	① ② ③ ④ ⑤ ⑥ ⑦ ⑧ ⑨ ⑩

HYPERACTIVITY

CONSTANTLY MOVING / TALKING	① ② ③ ④ ⑤ ⑥ ⑦ ⑧ ⑨ ⑩
STRUGGLING TO SIT STILL	① ② ③ ④ ⑤ ⑥ ⑦ ⑧ ⑨ ⑩
TOUCHING THINGS REPEATEDLY	① ② ③ ④ ⑤ ⑥ ⑦ ⑧ ⑨ ⑩
DIFFICULT SLEEPING	① ② ③ ④ ⑤ ⑥ ⑦ ⑧ ⑨ ⑩

IMPULSIVITY

ACTING WITHOUT THINKING	① ② ③ ④ ⑤ ⑥ ⑦ ⑧ ⑨ ⑩
INTERRUPTING OTHERS	① ② ③ ④ ⑤ ⑥ ⑦ ⑧ ⑨ ⑩
EASILY FRUSTRATED	① ② ③ ④ ⑤ ⑥ ⑦ ⑧ ⑨ ⑩
UNABLE TO HOLD BACKE MOTIONS	① ② ③ ④ ⑤ ⑥ ⑦ ⑧ ⑨ ⑩

MEALS

MEDICATIONS

WATER TRACKER

NOTES

....

....

DAY GOALS

1 ....
2 ....
3 ....

DATE

WEEK

LOCATION

WEIGHT

MOOD TRACKER

BEHAVIOR

INATTENTION

SHORT ATTENTION	① ② ③ ④ ⑤ ⑥ ⑦ ⑧ ⑨ ⑩
UNMOTIVATED / BORED	① ② ③ ④ ⑤ ⑥ ⑦ ⑧ ⑨ ⑩
SHORT ATTENTION	① ② ③ ④ ⑤ ⑥ ⑦ ⑧ ⑨ ⑩
FORGETFUL / CONFUSIONED	① ② ③ ④ ⑤ ⑥ ⑦ ⑧ ⑨ ⑩

HYPERACTIVITY

CONSTANTLY MOVING / TALKING	① ② ③ ④ ⑤ ⑥ ⑦ ⑧ ⑨ ⑩
STRUGGLING TO SIT STILL	① ② ③ ④ ⑤ ⑥ ⑦ ⑧ ⑨ ⑩
TOUCHING THINGS REPEATEDLY	① ② ③ ④ ⑤ ⑥ ⑦ ⑧ ⑨ ⑩
DIFFICULT SLEEPING	① ② ③ ④ ⑤ ⑥ ⑦ ⑧ ⑨ ⑩

IMPULSIVITY

ACTING WITHOUT THINKING	① ② ③ ④ ⑤ ⑥ ⑦ ⑧ ⑨ ⑩
INTERRUPTING OTHERS	① ② ③ ④ ⑤ ⑥ ⑦ ⑧ ⑨ ⑩
EASILY FRUSTRATED	① ② ③ ④ ⑤ ⑥ ⑦ ⑧ ⑨ ⑩
UNABLE TO HOLD BACKE MOTIONS	① ② ③ ④ ⑤ ⑥ ⑦ ⑧ ⑨ ⑩

MEALS

MEDICATIONS

WATER TRACKER

NOTES

....
....

DAY GOALS

1 ....
2 ....
3 ....

DATE

WEEK

LOCATION

WEIGHT

MOOD TRACKER

😕 😐 😖 😢 😠 😃

BEHAVIOR

INATTENTION

SHORT ATTENTION	① ② ③ ④ ⑤ ⑥ ⑦ ⑧ ⑨ ⑩
UNMOTIVATED / BORED	① ② ③ ④ ⑤ ⑥ ⑦ ⑧ ⑨ ⑩
SHORT ATTENTION	① ② ③ ④ ⑤ ⑥ ⑦ ⑧ ⑨ ⑩
FORGETFUL / CONFUSIONED	① ② ③ ④ ⑤ ⑥ ⑦ ⑧ ⑨ ⑩

HYPERACTIVITY

CONSTANTLY MOVING / TALKING	① ② ③ ④ ⑤ ⑥ ⑦ ⑧ ⑨ ⑩
STRUGGLING TO SIT STILL	① ② ③ ④ ⑤ ⑥ ⑦ ⑧ ⑨ ⑩
TOUCHING THINGS REPEATEDLY	① ② ③ ④ ⑤ ⑥ ⑦ ⑧ ⑨ ⑩
DIFFICULT SLEEPING	① ② ③ ④ ⑤ ⑥ ⑦ ⑧ ⑨ ⑩

IMPULSIVITY

ACTING WITHOUT THINKING	① ② ③ ④ ⑤ ⑥ ⑦ ⑧ ⑨ ⑩
INTERRUPTING OTHERS	① ② ③ ④ ⑤ ⑥ ⑦ ⑧ ⑨ ⑩
EASILY FRUSTRATED	① ② ③ ④ ⑤ ⑥ ⑦ ⑧ ⑨ ⑩
UNABLE TO HOLD BACKE MOTIONS	① ② ③ ④ ⑤ ⑥ ⑦ ⑧ ⑨ ⑩

MEALS

MEDICATIONS

WATER TRACKER

NOTES

....
....

DAY GOALS

1 ....
2 ....
3 ....

DATE
WEEK
LOCATION
WEIGHT

MOOD TRACKER

BEHAVIOR

INATTENTION

SHORT ATTENTION	① ② ③ ④ ⑤ ⑥ ⑦ ⑧ ⑨ ⑩
UNMOTIVATED / BORED	① ② ③ ④ ⑤ ⑥ ⑦ ⑧ ⑨ ⑩
SHORT ATTENTION	① ② ③ ④ ⑤ ⑥ ⑦ ⑧ ⑨ ⑩
FORGETFUL / CONFUSIONED	① ② ③ ④ ⑤ ⑥ ⑦ ⑧ ⑨ ⑩

HYPERACTIVITY

CONSTANTLY MOVING / TALKING	① ② ③ ④ ⑤ ⑥ ⑦ ⑧ ⑨ ⑩
STRUGGLING TO SIT STILL	① ② ③ ④ ⑤ ⑥ ⑦ ⑧ ⑨ ⑩
TOUCHING THINGS REPEATEDLY	① ② ③ ④ ⑤ ⑥ ⑦ ⑧ ⑨ ⑩
DIFFICULT SLEEPING	① ② ③ ④ ⑤ ⑥ ⑦ ⑧ ⑨ ⑩

IMPULSIVITY

ACTING WITHOUT THINKING	① ② ③ ④ ⑤ ⑥ ⑦ ⑧ ⑨ ⑩
INTERRUPTING OTHERS	① ② ③ ④ ⑤ ⑥ ⑦ ⑧ ⑨ ⑩
EASILY FRUSTRATED	① ② ③ ④ ⑤ ⑥ ⑦ ⑧ ⑨ ⑩
UNABLE TO HOLD BACKE MOTIONS	① ② ③ ④ ⑤ ⑥ ⑦ ⑧ ⑨ ⑩

MEALS

MEDICATIONS

WATER TRACKER

NOTES

....
....

MOOD TRACKER ☹ 😐 😣 😢 😠 😃

BEHAVIOR

INATTENTION

SHORT ATTENTION	① ② ③ ④ ⑤ ⑥ ⑦ ⑧ ⑨ ⑩
UNMOTIVATED / BORED	① ② ③ ④ ⑤ ⑥ ⑦ ⑧ ⑨ ⑩
SHORT ATTENTION	① ② ③ ④ ⑤ ⑥ ⑦ ⑧ ⑨ ⑩
FORGETFUL / CONFUSIONED	① ② ③ ④ ⑤ ⑥ ⑦ ⑧ ⑨ ⑩

HYPERACTIVITY

CONSTANTLY MOVING / TALKING	① ② ③ ④ ⑤ ⑥ ⑦ ⑧ ⑨ ⑩
STRUGGLING TO SIT STILL	① ② ③ ④ ⑤ ⑥ ⑦ ⑧ ⑨ ⑩
TOUCHING THINGS REPEATEDLY	① ② ③ ④ ⑤ ⑥ ⑦ ⑧ ⑨ ⑩
DIFFICULT SLEEPING	① ② ③ ④ ⑤ ⑥ ⑦ ⑧ ⑨ ⑩

IMPULSIVITY

ACTING WITHOUT THINKING	① ② ③ ④ ⑤ ⑥ ⑦ ⑧ ⑨ ⑩
INTERRUPTING OTHERS	① ② ③ ④ ⑤ ⑥ ⑦ ⑧ ⑨ ⑩
EASILY FRUSTRATED	① ② ③ ④ ⑤ ⑥ ⑦ ⑧ ⑨ ⑩
UNABLE TO HOLD BACKE MOTIONS	① ② ③ ④ ⑤ ⑥ ⑦ ⑧ ⑨ ⑩

MEALS

MEDICATIONS

WATER TRACKER ⬜ ⬜ ⬜ ⬜ ⬜ ⬜ ⬜

NOTES

....

....

DAY GOALS

1 ....
2 ....
3 ....

DATE

WEEK

LOCATION

WEIGHT

MOOD TRACKER ☹ 😐 😖 😢 😠 😃

BEHAVIOR

INATTENTION

SHORT ATTENTION	① ② ③ ④ ⑤ ⑥ ⑦ ⑧ ⑨ ⑩
UNMOTIVATED / BORED	① ② ③ ④ ⑤ ⑥ ⑦ ⑧ ⑨ ⑩
SHORT ATTENTION	① ② ③ ④ ⑤ ⑥ ⑦ ⑧ ⑨ ⑩
FORGETFUL / CONFUSIONED	① ② ③ ④ ⑤ ⑥ ⑦ ⑧ ⑨ ⑩

HYPERACTIVITY

CONSTANTLY MOVING / TALKING	① ② ③ ④ ⑤ ⑥ ⑦ ⑧ ⑨ ⑩
STRUGGLING TO SIT STILL	① ② ③ ④ ⑤ ⑥ ⑦ ⑧ ⑨ ⑩
TOUCHING THINGS REPEATEDLY	① ② ③ ④ ⑤ ⑥ ⑦ ⑧ ⑨ ⑩
DIFFICULT SLEEPING	① ② ③ ④ ⑤ ⑥ ⑦ ⑧ ⑨ ⑩

IMPULSIVITY

ACTING WITHOUT THINKING	① ② ③ ④ ⑤ ⑥ ⑦ ⑧ ⑨ ⑩
INTERRUPTING OTHERS	① ② ③ ④ ⑤ ⑥ ⑦ ⑧ ⑨ ⑩
EASILY FRUSTRATED	① ② ③ ④ ⑤ ⑥ ⑦ ⑧ ⑨ ⑩
UNABLE TO HOLD BACKE MOTIONS	① ② ③ ④ ⑤ ⑥ ⑦ ⑧ ⑨ ⑩

MEALS

MEDICATIONS

WATER TRACKER 🥛 🥛 🥛 🥛 🥛 🥛 🥛

NOTES

....
....

MOOD TRACKER   :(:| >< :'(>:(:D

BEHAVIOR

INATTENTION

SHORT ATTENTION	① ② ③ ④ ⑤ ⑥ ⑦ ⑧ ⑨ ⑩
UNMOTIVATED / BORED	① ② ③ ④ ⑤ ⑥ ⑦ ⑧ ⑨ ⑩
SHORT ATTENTION	① ② ③ ④ ⑤ ⑥ ⑦ ⑧ ⑨ ⑩
FORGETFUL / CONFUSIONED	① ② ③ ④ ⑤ ⑥ ⑦ ⑧ ⑨ ⑩

HYPERACTIVITY

CONSTANTLY MOVING / TALKING	① ② ③ ④ ⑤ ⑥ ⑦ ⑧ ⑨ ⑩
STRUGGLING TO SIT STILL	① ② ③ ④ ⑤ ⑥ ⑦ ⑧ ⑨ ⑩
TOUCHING THINGS REPEATEDLY	① ② ③ ④ ⑤ ⑥ ⑦ ⑧ ⑨ ⑩
DIFFICULT SLEEPING	① ② ③ ④ ⑤ ⑥ ⑦ ⑧ ⑨ ⑩

IMPULSIVITY

ACTING WITHOUT THINKING	① ② ③ ④ ⑤ ⑥ ⑦ ⑧ ⑨ ⑩
INTERRUPTING OTHERS	① ② ③ ④ ⑤ ⑥ ⑦ ⑧ ⑨ ⑩
EASILY FRUSTRATED	① ② ③ ④ ⑤ ⑥ ⑦ ⑧ ⑨ ⑩
UNABLE TO HOLD BACKE MOTIONS	① ② ③ ④ ⑤ ⑥ ⑦ ⑧ ⑨ ⑩

MEALS

MEDICATIONS

WATER TRACKER ⌵ ⌵ ⌵ ⌵ ⌵ ⌵ ⌵

NOTES

....
....

DAY GOALS

1 ....
2 ....
3 ....

DATE

WEEK

LOCATION

WEIGHT

MOOD TRACKER

BEHAVIOR

INATTENTION

SHORT ATTENTION	① ② ③ ④ ⑤ ⑥ ⑦ ⑧ ⑨ ⑩
UNMOTIVATED / BORED	① ② ③ ④ ⑤ ⑥ ⑦ ⑧ ⑨ ⑩
SHORT ATTENTION	① ② ③ ④ ⑤ ⑥ ⑦ ⑧ ⑨ ⑩
FORGETFUL / CONFUSIONED	① ② ③ ④ ⑤ ⑥ ⑦ ⑧ ⑨ ⑩

HYPERACTIVITY

CONSTANTLY MOVING / TALKING	① ② ③ ④ ⑤ ⑥ ⑦ ⑧ ⑨ ⑩
STRUGGLING TO SIT STILL	① ② ③ ④ ⑤ ⑥ ⑦ ⑧ ⑨ ⑩
TOUCHING THINGS REPEATEDLY	① ② ③ ④ ⑤ ⑥ ⑦ ⑧ ⑨ ⑩
DIFFICULT SLEEPING	① ② ③ ④ ⑤ ⑥ ⑦ ⑧ ⑨ ⑩

IMPULSIVITY

ACTING WITHOUT THINKING	① ② ③ ④ ⑤ ⑥ ⑦ ⑧ ⑨ ⑩
INTERRUPTING OTHERS	① ② ③ ④ ⑤ ⑥ ⑦ ⑧ ⑨ ⑩
EASILY FRUSTRATED	① ② ③ ④ ⑤ ⑥ ⑦ ⑧ ⑨ ⑩
UNABLE TO HOLD BACKE MOTIONS	① ② ③ ④ ⑤ ⑥ ⑦ ⑧ ⑨ ⑩

MEALS

MEDICATIONS

WATER TRACKER

NOTES

....
....

DAY GOALS

1 ....
2 ....
3 ....

DATE

WEEK

LOCATION

WEIGHT

MOOD TRACKER

BEHAVIOR

INATTENTION

SHORT ATTENTION	① ② ③ ④ ⑤ ⑥ ⑦ ⑧ ⑨ ⑩
UNMOTIVATED / BORED	① ② ③ ④ ⑤ ⑥ ⑦ ⑧ ⑨ ⑩
SHORT ATTENTION	① ② ③ ④ ⑤ ⑥ ⑦ ⑧ ⑨ ⑩
FORGETFUL / CONFUSIONED	① ② ③ ④ ⑤ ⑥ ⑦ ⑧ ⑨ ⑩

HYPERACTIVITY

CONSTANTLY MOVING / TALKING	① ② ③ ④ ⑤ ⑥ ⑦ ⑧ ⑨ ⑩
STRUGGLING TO SIT STILL	① ② ③ ④ ⑤ ⑥ ⑦ ⑧ ⑨ ⑩
TOUCHING THINGS REPEATEDLY	① ② ③ ④ ⑤ ⑥ ⑦ ⑧ ⑨ ⑩
DIFFICULT SLEEPING	① ② ③ ④ ⑤ ⑥ ⑦ ⑧ ⑨ ⑩

IMPULSIVITY

ACTING WITHOUT THINKING	① ② ③ ④ ⑤ ⑥ ⑦ ⑧ ⑨ ⑩
INTERRUPTING OTHERS	① ② ③ ④ ⑤ ⑥ ⑦ ⑧ ⑨ ⑩
EASILY FRUSTRATED	① ② ③ ④ ⑤ ⑥ ⑦ ⑧ ⑨ ⑩
UNABLE TO HOLD BACKE MOTIONS	① ② ③ ④ ⑤ ⑥ ⑦ ⑧ ⑨ ⑩

MEALS

MEDICATIONS

WATER TRACKER

NOTES

....
....

MOOD TRACKER

BEHAVIOR

INATTENTION

SHORT ATTENTION	① ② ③ ④ ⑤ ⑥ ⑦ ⑧ ⑨ ⑩
UNMOTIVATED / BORED	① ② ③ ④ ⑤ ⑥ ⑦ ⑧ ⑨ ⑩
SHORT ATTENTION	① ② ③ ④ ⑤ ⑥ ⑦ ⑧ ⑨ ⑩
FORGETFUL / CONFUSIONED	① ② ③ ④ ⑤ ⑥ ⑦ ⑧ ⑨ ⑩

HYPERACTIVITY

CONSTANTLY MOVING / TALKING	① ② ③ ④ ⑤ ⑥ ⑦ ⑧ ⑨ ⑩
STRUGGLING TO SIT STILL	① ② ③ ④ ⑤ ⑥ ⑦ ⑧ ⑨ ⑩
TOUCHING THINGS REPEATEDLY	① ② ③ ④ ⑤ ⑥ ⑦ ⑧ ⑨ ⑩
DIFFICULT SLEEPING	① ② ③ ④ ⑤ ⑥ ⑦ ⑧ ⑨ ⑩

IMPULSIVITY

ACTING WITHOUT THINKING	① ② ③ ④ ⑤ ⑥ ⑦ ⑧ ⑨ ⑩
INTERRUPTING OTHERS	① ② ③ ④ ⑤ ⑥ ⑦ ⑧ ⑨ ⑩
EASILY FRUSTRATED	① ② ③ ④ ⑤ ⑥ ⑦ ⑧ ⑨ ⑩
UNABLE TO HOLD BACKE MOTIONS	① ② ③ ④ ⑤ ⑥ ⑦ ⑧ ⑨ ⑩

MEALS

MEDICATIONS

WATER TRACKER

NOTES

....
....

DAY GOALS

1 ....
2 ....
3 ....

MOOD TRACKER

BEHAVIOR

INATTENTION

SHORT ATTENTION	① ② ③ ④ ⑤ ⑥ ⑦ ⑧ ⑨ ⑩
UNMOTIVATED / BORED	① ② ③ ④ ⑤ ⑥ ⑦ ⑧ ⑨ ⑩
SHORT ATTENTION	① ② ③ ④ ⑤ ⑥ ⑦ ⑧ ⑨ ⑩
FORGETFUL / CONFUSIONED	① ② ③ ④ ⑤ ⑥ ⑦ ⑧ ⑨ ⑩

HYPERACTIVITY

CONSTANTLY MOVING / TALKING	① ② ③ ④ ⑤ ⑥ ⑦ ⑧ ⑨ ⑩
STRUGGLING TO SIT STILL	① ② ③ ④ ⑤ ⑥ ⑦ ⑧ ⑨ ⑩
TOUCHING THINGS REPEATEDLY	① ② ③ ④ ⑤ ⑥ ⑦ ⑧ ⑨ ⑩
DIFFICULT SLEEPING	① ② ③ ④ ⑤ ⑥ ⑦ ⑧ ⑨ ⑩

IMPULSIVITY

ACTING WITHOUT THINKING	① ② ③ ④ ⑤ ⑥ ⑦ ⑧ ⑨ ⑩
INTERRUPTING OTHERS	① ② ③ ④ ⑤ ⑥ ⑦ ⑧ ⑨ ⑩
EASILY FRUSTRATED	① ② ③ ④ ⑤ ⑥ ⑦ ⑧ ⑨ ⑩
UNABLE TO HOLD BACKE MOTIONS	① ② ③ ④ ⑤ ⑥ ⑦ ⑧ ⑨ ⑩

MEALS

MEDICATIONS

WATER TRACKER

NOTES

....
....

MOOD TRACKER

BEHAVIOR

INATTENTION

SHORT ATTENTION	① ② ③ ④ ⑤ ⑥ ⑦ ⑧ ⑨ ⑩
UNMOTIVATED / BORED	① ② ③ ④ ⑤ ⑥ ⑦ ⑧ ⑨ ⑩
SHORT ATTENTION	① ② ③ ④ ⑤ ⑥ ⑦ ⑧ ⑨ ⑩
FORGETFUL / CONFUSIONED	① ② ③ ④ ⑤ ⑥ ⑦ ⑧ ⑨ ⑩

HYPERACTIVITY

CONSTANTLY MOVING / TALKING	① ② ③ ④ ⑤ ⑥ ⑦ ⑧ ⑨ ⑩
STRUGGLING TO SIT STILL	① ② ③ ④ ⑤ ⑥ ⑦ ⑧ ⑨ ⑩
TOUCHING THINGS REPEATEDLY	① ② ③ ④ ⑤ ⑥ ⑦ ⑧ ⑨ ⑩
DIFFICULT SLEEPING	① ② ③ ④ ⑤ ⑥ ⑦ ⑧ ⑨ ⑩

IMPULSIVITY

ACTING WITHOUT THINKING	① ② ③ ④ ⑤ ⑥ ⑦ ⑧ ⑨ ⑩
INTERRUPTING OTHERS	① ② ③ ④ ⑤ ⑥ ⑦ ⑧ ⑨ ⑩
EASILY FRUSTRATED	① ② ③ ④ ⑤ ⑥ ⑦ ⑧ ⑨ ⑩
UNABLE TO HOLD BACKE MOTIONS	① ② ③ ④ ⑤ ⑥ ⑦ ⑧ ⑨ ⑩

MEALS	MEDICATIONS

WATER TRACKER

NOTES

....
....

MOOD TRACKER (·‿·) (·_·) (>‿<) (·﹏·) (ˋ﹏ˊ) (◡‿◡)

BEHAVIOR

INATTENTION

SHORT ATTENTION	① ② ③ ④ ⑤ ⑥ ⑦ ⑧ ⑨ ⑩
UNMOTIVATED / BORED	① ② ③ ④ ⑤ ⑥ ⑦ ⑧ ⑨ ⑩
SHORT ATTENTION	① ② ③ ④ ⑤ ⑥ ⑦ ⑧ ⑨ ⑩
FORGETFUL / CONFUSIONED	① ② ③ ④ ⑤ ⑥ ⑦ ⑧ ⑨ ⑩

HYPERACTIVITY

CONSTANTLY MOVING / TALKING	① ② ③ ④ ⑤ ⑥ ⑦ ⑧ ⑨ ⑩
STRUGGLING TO SIT STILL	① ② ③ ④ ⑤ ⑥ ⑦ ⑧ ⑨ ⑩
TOUCHING THINGS REPEATEDLY	① ② ③ ④ ⑤ ⑥ ⑦ ⑧ ⑨ ⑩
DIFFICULT SLEEPING	① ② ③ ④ ⑤ ⑥ ⑦ ⑧ ⑨ ⑩

IMPULSIVITY

ACTING WITHOUT THINKING	① ② ③ ④ ⑤ ⑥ ⑦ ⑧ ⑨ ⑩
INTERRUPTING OTHERS	① ② ③ ④ ⑤ ⑥ ⑦ ⑧ ⑨ ⑩
EASILY FRUSTRATED	① ② ③ ④ ⑤ ⑥ ⑦ ⑧ ⑨ ⑩
UNABLE TO HOLD BACKE MOTIONS	① ② ③ ④ ⑤ ⑥ ⑦ ⑧ ⑨ ⑩

MEALS | MEDICATIONS

WATER TRACKER ⛶ ⛶ ⛶ ⛶ ⛶ ⛶ ⛶

NOTES

....
....
....

DAY GOALS

1 ....
2 ....
3 ....

DATE

WEEK

LOCATION

WEIGHT

MOOD TRACKER 😟 😐 😣 😢 😠 😃

BEHAVIOR

INATTENTION

SHORT ATTENTION	① ② ③ ④ ⑤ ⑥ ⑦ ⑧ ⑨ ⑩
UNMOTIVATED / BORED	① ② ③ ④ ⑤ ⑥ ⑦ ⑧ ⑨ ⑩
SHORT ATTENTION	① ② ③ ④ ⑤ ⑥ ⑦ ⑧ ⑨ ⑩
FORGETFUL / CONFUSIONED	① ② ③ ④ ⑤ ⑥ ⑦ ⑧ ⑨ ⑩

HYPERACTIVITY

CONSTANTLY MOVING / TALKING	① ② ③ ④ ⑤ ⑥ ⑦ ⑧ ⑨ ⑩
STRUGGLING TO SIT STILL	① ② ③ ④ ⑤ ⑥ ⑦ ⑧ ⑨ ⑩
TOUCHING THINGS REPEATEDLY	① ② ③ ④ ⑤ ⑥ ⑦ ⑧ ⑨ ⑩
DIFFICULT SLEEPING	① ② ③ ④ ⑤ ⑥ ⑦ ⑧ ⑨ ⑩

IMPULSIVITY

ACTING WITHOUT THINKING	① ② ③ ④ ⑤ ⑥ ⑦ ⑧ ⑨ ⑩
INTERRUPTING OTHERS	① ② ③ ④ ⑤ ⑥ ⑦ ⑧ ⑨ ⑩
EASILY FRUSTRATED	① ② ③ ④ ⑤ ⑥ ⑦ ⑧ ⑨ ⑩
UNABLE TO HOLD BACKE MOTIONS	① ② ③ ④ ⑤ ⑥ ⑦ ⑧ ⑨ ⑩

MEALS

MEDICATIONS

WATER TRACKER ⬜ ⬜ ⬜ ⬜ ⬜ ⬜ ⬜

NOTES

....
....

DAY GOALS

1 ....
2 ....
3 ....

DATE
WEEK
LOCATION
WEIGHT

MOOD TRACKER

BEHAVIOR

INATTENTION

SHORT ATTENTION	① ② ③ ④ ⑤ ⑥ ⑦ ⑧ ⑨ ⑩
UNMOTIVATED / BORED	① ② ③ ④ ⑤ ⑥ ⑦ ⑧ ⑨ ⑩
SHORT ATTENTION	① ② ③ ④ ⑤ ⑥ ⑦ ⑧ ⑨ ⑩
FORGETFUL / CONFUSIONED	① ② ③ ④ ⑤ ⑥ ⑦ ⑧ ⑨ ⑩

HYPERACTIVITY

CONSTANTLY MOVING / TALKING	① ② ③ ④ ⑤ ⑥ ⑦ ⑧ ⑨ ⑩
STRUGGLING TO SIT STILL	① ② ③ ④ ⑤ ⑥ ⑦ ⑧ ⑨ ⑩
TOUCHING THINGS REPEATEDLY	① ② ③ ④ ⑤ ⑥ ⑦ ⑧ ⑨ ⑩
DIFFICULT SLEEPING	① ② ③ ④ ⑤ ⑥ ⑦ ⑧ ⑨ ⑩

IMPULSIVITY

ACTING WITHOUT THINKING	① ② ③ ④ ⑤ ⑥ ⑦ ⑧ ⑨ ⑩
INTERRUPTING OTHERS	① ② ③ ④ ⑤ ⑥ ⑦ ⑧ ⑨ ⑩
EASILY FRUSTRATED	① ② ③ ④ ⑤ ⑥ ⑦ ⑧ ⑨ ⑩
UNABLE TO HOLD BACKE MOTIONS	① ② ③ ④ ⑤ ⑥ ⑦ ⑧ ⑨ ⑩

MEALS

MEDICATIONS

WATER TRACKER

NOTES

....
....

DAY GOALS

1 ....
2 ....
3 ....

DATE

WEEK

LOCATION

WEIGHT

MOOD TRACKER

BEHAVIOR

INATTENTION

SHORT ATTENTION	① ② ③ ④ ⑤ ⑥ ⑦ ⑧ ⑨ ⑩
UNMOTIVATED / BORED	① ② ③ ④ ⑤ ⑥ ⑦ ⑧ ⑨ ⑩
SHORT ATTENTION	① ② ③ ④ ⑤ ⑥ ⑦ ⑧ ⑨ ⑩
FORGETFUL / CONFUSIONED	① ② ③ ④ ⑤ ⑥ ⑦ ⑧ ⑨ ⑩

HYPERACTIVITY

CONSTANTLY MOVING / TALKING	① ② ③ ④ ⑤ ⑥ ⑦ ⑧ ⑨ ⑩
STRUGGLING TO SIT STILL	① ② ③ ④ ⑤ ⑥ ⑦ ⑧ ⑨ ⑩
TOUCHING THINGS REPEATEDLY	① ② ③ ④ ⑤ ⑥ ⑦ ⑧ ⑨ ⑩
DIFFICULT SLEEPING	① ② ③ ④ ⑤ ⑥ ⑦ ⑧ ⑨ ⑩

IMPULSIVITY

ACTING WITHOUT THINKING	① ② ③ ④ ⑤ ⑥ ⑦ ⑧ ⑨ ⑩
INTERRUPTING OTHERS	① ② ③ ④ ⑤ ⑥ ⑦ ⑧ ⑨ ⑩
EASILY FRUSTRATED	① ② ③ ④ ⑤ ⑥ ⑦ ⑧ ⑨ ⑩
UNABLE TO HOLD BACKE MOTIONS	① ② ③ ④ ⑤ ⑥ ⑦ ⑧ ⑨ ⑩

MEALS

MEDICATIONS

WATER TRACKER

NOTES

....
....

MOOD TRACKER

BEHAVIOR

INATTENTION

SHORT ATTENTION	① ② ③ ④ ⑤ ⑥ ⑦ ⑧ ⑨ ⑩
UNMOTIVATED / BORED	① ② ③ ④ ⑤ ⑥ ⑦ ⑧ ⑨ ⑩
SHORT ATTENTION	① ② ③ ④ ⑤ ⑥ ⑦ ⑧ ⑨ ⑩
FORGETFUL / CONFUSIONED	① ② ③ ④ ⑤ ⑥ ⑦ ⑧ ⑨ ⑩

HYPERACTIVITY

CONSTANTLY MOVING / TALKING	① ② ③ ④ ⑤ ⑥ ⑦ ⑧ ⑨ ⑩
STRUGGLING TO SIT STILL	① ② ③ ④ ⑤ ⑥ ⑦ ⑧ ⑨ ⑩
TOUCHING THINGS REPEATEDLY	① ② ③ ④ ⑤ ⑥ ⑦ ⑧ ⑨ ⑩
DIFFICULT SLEEPING	① ② ③ ④ ⑤ ⑥ ⑦ ⑧ ⑨ ⑩

IMPULSIVITY

ACTING WITHOUT THINKING	① ② ③ ④ ⑤ ⑥ ⑦ ⑧ ⑨ ⑩
INTERRUPTING OTHERS	① ② ③ ④ ⑤ ⑥ ⑦ ⑧ ⑨ ⑩
EASILY FRUSTRATED	① ② ③ ④ ⑤ ⑥ ⑦ ⑧ ⑨ ⑩
UNABLE TO HOLD BACKE MOTIONS	① ② ③ ④ ⑤ ⑥ ⑦ ⑧ ⑨ ⑩

MEALS

MEDICATIONS

WATER TRACKER

NOTES

....

....

DAY GOALS

1 ....
2 ....
3 ....

DATE
WEEK
LOCATION
WEIGHT

MOOD TRACKER

BEHAVIOR

INATTENTION

SHORT ATTENTION	① ② ③ ④ ⑤ ⑥ ⑦ ⑧ ⑨ ⑩
UNMOTIVATED / BORED	① ② ③ ④ ⑤ ⑥ ⑦ ⑧ ⑨ ⑩
SHORT ATTENTION	① ② ③ ④ ⑤ ⑥ ⑦ ⑧ ⑨ ⑩
FORGETFUL / CONFUSIONED	① ② ③ ④ ⑤ ⑥ ⑦ ⑧ ⑨ ⑩

HYPERACTIVITY

CONSTANTLY MOVING / TALKING	① ② ③ ④ ⑤ ⑥ ⑦ ⑧ ⑨ ⑩
STRUGGLING TO SIT STILL	① ② ③ ④ ⑤ ⑥ ⑦ ⑧ ⑨ ⑩
TOUCHING THINGS REPEATEDLY	① ② ③ ④ ⑤ ⑥ ⑦ ⑧ ⑨ ⑩
DIFFICULT SLEEPING	① ② ③ ④ ⑤ ⑥ ⑦ ⑧ ⑨ ⑩

IMPULSIVITY

ACTING WITHOUT THINKING	① ② ③ ④ ⑤ ⑥ ⑦ ⑧ ⑨ ⑩
INTERRUPTING OTHERS	① ② ③ ④ ⑤ ⑥ ⑦ ⑧ ⑨ ⑩
EASILY FRUSTRATED	① ② ③ ④ ⑤ ⑥ ⑦ ⑧ ⑨ ⑩
UNABLE TO HOLD BACKE MOTIONS	① ② ③ ④ ⑤ ⑥ ⑦ ⑧ ⑨ ⑩

MEALS

MEDICATIONS

WATER TRACKER

NOTES

....
....

DAY GOALS

1 ....
2 ....
3 ....

DATE

WEEK

LOCATION

WEIGHT

MOOD TRACKER

BEHAVIOR

INATTENTION

SHORT ATTENTION	① ② ③ ④ ⑤ ⑥ ⑦ ⑧ ⑨ ⑩
UNMOTIVATED / BORED	① ② ③ ④ ⑤ ⑥ ⑦ ⑧ ⑨ ⑩
SHORT ATTENTION	① ② ③ ④ ⑤ ⑥ ⑦ ⑧ ⑨ ⑩
FORGETFUL / CONFUSIONED	① ② ③ ④ ⑤ ⑥ ⑦ ⑧ ⑨ ⑩

HYPERACTIVITY

CONSTANTLY MOVING / TALKING	① ② ③ ④ ⑤ ⑥ ⑦ ⑧ ⑨ ⑩
STRUGGLING TO SIT STILL	① ② ③ ④ ⑤ ⑥ ⑦ ⑧ ⑨ ⑩
TOUCHING THINGS REPEATEDLY	① ② ③ ④ ⑤ ⑥ ⑦ ⑧ ⑨ ⑩
DIFFICULT SLEEPING	① ② ③ ④ ⑤ ⑥ ⑦ ⑧ ⑨ ⑩

IMPULSIVITY

ACTING WITHOUT THINKING	① ② ③ ④ ⑤ ⑥ ⑦ ⑧ ⑨ ⑩
INTERRUPTING OTHERS	① ② ③ ④ ⑤ ⑥ ⑦ ⑧ ⑨ ⑩
EASILY FRUSTRATED	① ② ③ ④ ⑤ ⑥ ⑦ ⑧ ⑨ ⑩
UNABLE TO HOLD BACKE MOTIONS	① ② ③ ④ ⑤ ⑥ ⑦ ⑧ ⑨ ⑩

MEALS

MEDICATIONS

WATER TRACKER

NOTES

....
....

DAY GOALS

1 ....
2 ....
3 ....

DATE

WEEK

LOCATION

WEIGHT

MOOD TRACKER

BEHAVIOR

INATTENTION

SHORT ATTENTION	① ② ③ ④ ⑤ ⑥ ⑦ ⑧ ⑨ ⑩
UNMOTIVATED / BORED	① ② ③ ④ ⑤ ⑥ ⑦ ⑧ ⑨ ⑩
SHORT ATTENTION	① ② ③ ④ ⑤ ⑥ ⑦ ⑧ ⑨ ⑩
FORGETFUL / CONFUSIONED	① ② ③ ④ ⑤ ⑥ ⑦ ⑧ ⑨ ⑩

HYPERACTIVITY

CONSTANTLY MOVING / TALKING	① ② ③ ④ ⑤ ⑥ ⑦ ⑧ ⑨ ⑩
STRUGGLING TO SIT STILL	① ② ③ ④ ⑤ ⑥ ⑦ ⑧ ⑨ ⑩
TOUCHING THINGS REPEATEDLY	① ② ③ ④ ⑤ ⑥ ⑦ ⑧ ⑨ ⑩
DIFFICULT SLEEPING	① ② ③ ④ ⑤ ⑥ ⑦ ⑧ ⑨ ⑩

IMPULSIVITY

ACTING WITHOUT THINKING	① ② ③ ④ ⑤ ⑥ ⑦ ⑧ ⑨ ⑩
INTERRUPTING OTHERS	① ② ③ ④ ⑤ ⑥ ⑦ ⑧ ⑨ ⑩
EASILY FRUSTRATED	① ② ③ ④ ⑤ ⑥ ⑦ ⑧ ⑨ ⑩
UNABLE TO HOLD BACKE MOTIONS	① ② ③ ④ ⑤ ⑥ ⑦ ⑧ ⑨ ⑩

MEALS

MEDICATIONS

WATER TRACKER

NOTES

....
....

DAY GOALS

1 ....
2 ....
3 ....

DATE

WEEK

LOCATION

WEIGHT

MOOD TRACKER

BEHAVIOR

INATTENTION

SHORT ATTENTION	① ② ③ ④ ⑤ ⑥ ⑦ ⑧ ⑨ ⑩
UNMOTIVATED / BORED	① ② ③ ④ ⑤ ⑥ ⑦ ⑧ ⑨ ⑩
SHORT ATTENTION	① ② ③ ④ ⑤ ⑥ ⑦ ⑧ ⑨ ⑩
FORGETFUL / CONFUSIONED	① ② ③ ④ ⑤ ⑥ ⑦ ⑧ ⑨ ⑩

HYPERACTIVITY

CONSTANTLY MOVING / TALKING	① ② ③ ④ ⑤ ⑥ ⑦ ⑧ ⑨ ⑩
STRUGGLING TO SIT STILL	① ② ③ ④ ⑤ ⑥ ⑦ ⑧ ⑨ ⑩
TOUCHING THINGS REPEATEDLY	① ② ③ ④ ⑤ ⑥ ⑦ ⑧ ⑨ ⑩
DIFFICULT SLEEPING	① ② ③ ④ ⑤ ⑥ ⑦ ⑧ ⑨ ⑩

IMPULSIVITY

ACTING WITHOUT THINKING	① ② ③ ④ ⑤ ⑥ ⑦ ⑧ ⑨ ⑩
INTERRUPTING OTHERS	① ② ③ ④ ⑤ ⑥ ⑦ ⑧ ⑨ ⑩
EASILY FRUSTRATED	① ② ③ ④ ⑤ ⑥ ⑦ ⑧ ⑨ ⑩
UNABLE TO HOLD BACKE MOTIONS	① ② ③ ④ ⑤ ⑥ ⑦ ⑧ ⑨ ⑩

MEALS

MEDICATIONS

WATER TRACKER

NOTES

....
....

MOOD TRACKER

BEHAVIOR

INATTENTION

SHORT ATTENTION	① ② ③ ④ ⑤ ⑥ ⑦ ⑧ ⑨ ⑩
UNMOTIVATED / BORED	① ② ③ ④ ⑤ ⑥ ⑦ ⑧ ⑨ ⑩
SHORT ATTENTION	① ② ③ ④ ⑤ ⑥ ⑦ ⑧ ⑨ ⑩
FORGETFUL / CONFUSIONED	① ② ③ ④ ⑤ ⑥ ⑦ ⑧ ⑨ ⑩

HYPERACTIVITY

CONSTANTLY MOVING / TALKING	① ② ③ ④ ⑤ ⑥ ⑦ ⑧ ⑨ ⑩
STRUGGLING TO SIT STILL	① ② ③ ④ ⑤ ⑥ ⑦ ⑧ ⑨ ⑩
TOUCHING THINGS REPEATEDLY	① ② ③ ④ ⑤ ⑥ ⑦ ⑧ ⑨ ⑩
DIFFICULT SLEEPING	① ② ③ ④ ⑤ ⑥ ⑦ ⑧ ⑨ ⑩

IMPULSIVITY

ACTING WITHOUT THINKING	① ② ③ ④ ⑤ ⑥ ⑦ ⑧ ⑨ ⑩
INTERRUPTING OTHERS	① ② ③ ④ ⑤ ⑥ ⑦ ⑧ ⑨ ⑩
EASILY FRUSTRATED	① ② ③ ④ ⑤ ⑥ ⑦ ⑧ ⑨ ⑩
UNABLE TO HOLD BACKE MOTIONS	① ② ③ ④ ⑤ ⑥ ⑦ ⑧ ⑨ ⑩

MEALS

MEDICATIONS

WATER TRACKER

NOTES

....
....

DAY GOALS

1 ....
2 ....
3 ....

DATE
WEEK
LOCATION
WEIGHT

MOOD TRACKER

BEHAVIOR

INATTENTION

SHORT ATTENTION	① ② ③ ④ ⑤ ⑥ ⑦ ⑧ ⑨ ⑩
UNMOTIVATED / BORED	① ② ③ ④ ⑤ ⑥ ⑦ ⑧ ⑨ ⑩
SHORT ATTENTION	① ② ③ ④ ⑤ ⑥ ⑦ ⑧ ⑨ ⑩
FORGETFUL / CONFUSIONED	① ② ③ ④ ⑤ ⑥ ⑦ ⑧ ⑨ ⑩

HYPERACTIVITY

CONSTANTLY MOVING / TALKING	① ② ③ ④ ⑤ ⑥ ⑦ ⑧ ⑨ ⑩
STRUGGLING TO SIT STILL	① ② ③ ④ ⑤ ⑥ ⑦ ⑧ ⑨ ⑩
TOUCHING THINGS REPEATEDLY	① ② ③ ④ ⑤ ⑥ ⑦ ⑧ ⑨ ⑩
DIFFICULT SLEEPING	① ② ③ ④ ⑤ ⑥ ⑦ ⑧ ⑨ ⑩

IMPULSIVITY

ACTING WITHOUT THINKING	① ② ③ ④ ⑤ ⑥ ⑦ ⑧ ⑨ ⑩
INTERRUPTING OTHERS	① ② ③ ④ ⑤ ⑥ ⑦ ⑧ ⑨ ⑩
EASILY FRUSTRATED	① ② ③ ④ ⑤ ⑥ ⑦ ⑧ ⑨ ⑩
UNABLE TO HOLD BACKE MOTIONS	① ② ③ ④ ⑤ ⑥ ⑦ ⑧ ⑨ ⑩

MEALS

MEDICATIONS

WATER TRACKER

NOTES

....
....

DAY GOALS

1 ....
2 ....
3 ....

DATE

WEEK

LOCATION

WEIGHT

MOOD TRACKER

BEHAVIOR

INATTENTION

SHORT ATTENTION	① ② ③ ④ ⑤ ⑥ ⑦ ⑧ ⑨ ⑩
UNMOTIVATED / BORED	① ② ③ ④ ⑤ ⑥ ⑦ ⑧ ⑨ ⑩
SHORT ATTENTION	① ② ③ ④ ⑤ ⑥ ⑦ ⑧ ⑨ ⑩
FORGETFUL / CONFUSIONED	① ② ③ ④ ⑤ ⑥ ⑦ ⑧ ⑨ ⑩

HYPERACTIVITY

CONSTANTLY MOVING / TALKING	① ② ③ ④ ⑤ ⑥ ⑦ ⑧ ⑨ ⑩
STRUGGLING TO SIT STILL	① ② ③ ④ ⑤ ⑥ ⑦ ⑧ ⑨ ⑩
TOUCHING THINGS REPEATEDLY	① ② ③ ④ ⑤ ⑥ ⑦ ⑧ ⑨ ⑩
DIFFICULT SLEEPING	① ② ③ ④ ⑤ ⑥ ⑦ ⑧ ⑨ ⑩

IMPULSIVITY

ACTING WITHOUT THINKING	① ② ③ ④ ⑤ ⑥ ⑦ ⑧ ⑨ ⑩
INTERRUPTING OTHERS	① ② ③ ④ ⑤ ⑥ ⑦ ⑧ ⑨ ⑩
EASILY FRUSTRATED	① ② ③ ④ ⑤ ⑥ ⑦ ⑧ ⑨ ⑩
UNABLE TO HOLD BACKE MOTIONS	① ② ③ ④ ⑤ ⑥ ⑦ ⑧ ⑨ ⑩

MEALS

MEDICATIONS

WATER TRACKER

NOTES

....
....

DAY GOALS

1 ....
2 ....
3 ....

DATE
WEEK
LOCATION
WEIGHT

MOOD TRACKER

BEHAVIOR

INATTENTION

SHORT ATTENTION — ① ② ③ ④ ⑤ ⑥ ⑦ ⑧ ⑨ ⑩
UNMOTIVATED / BORED — ① ② ③ ④ ⑤ ⑥ ⑦ ⑧ ⑨ ⑩
SHORT ATTENTION — ① ② ③ ④ ⑤ ⑥ ⑦ ⑧ ⑨ ⑩
FORGETFUL / CONFUSIONED — ① ② ③ ④ ⑤ ⑥ ⑦ ⑧ ⑨ ⑩

HYPERACTIVITY

CONSTANTLY MOVING / TALKING — ① ② ③ ④ ⑤ ⑥ ⑦ ⑧ ⑨ ⑩
STRUGGLING TO SIT STILL — ① ② ③ ④ ⑤ ⑥ ⑦ ⑧ ⑨ ⑩
TOUCHING THINGS REPEATEDLY — ① ② ③ ④ ⑤ ⑥ ⑦ ⑧ ⑨ ⑩
DIFFICULT SLEEPING — ① ② ③ ④ ⑤ ⑥ ⑦ ⑧ ⑨ ⑩

IMPULSIVITY

ACTING WITHOUT THINKING — ① ② ③ ④ ⑤ ⑥ ⑦ ⑧ ⑨ ⑩
INTERRUPTING OTHERS — ① ② ③ ④ ⑤ ⑥ ⑦ ⑧ ⑨ ⑩
EASILY FRUSTRATED — ① ② ③ ④ ⑤ ⑥ ⑦ ⑧ ⑨ ⑩
UNABLE TO HOLD BACKE MOTIONS — ① ② ③ ④ ⑤ ⑥ ⑦ ⑧ ⑨ ⑩

MEALS

MEDICATIONS

WATER TRACKER

NOTES

....
....

DAY GOALS

1 ....
2 ....
3 ....

DATE

WEEK

LOCATION

WEIGHT

MOOD TRACKER

☹ 😐 >< 😢 😠 😄

BEHAVIOR

INATTENTION

SHORT ATTENTION	① ② ③ ④ ⑤ ⑥ ⑦ ⑧ ⑨ ⑩
UNMOTIVATED / BORED	① ② ③ ④ ⑤ ⑥ ⑦ ⑧ ⑨ ⑩
SHORT ATTENTION	① ② ③ ④ ⑤ ⑥ ⑦ ⑧ ⑨ ⑩
FORGETFUL / CONFUSIONED	① ② ③ ④ ⑤ ⑥ ⑦ ⑧ ⑨ ⑩

HYPERACTIVITY

CONSTANTLY MOVING / TALKING	① ② ③ ④ ⑤ ⑥ ⑦ ⑧ ⑨ ⑩
STRUGGLING TO SIT STILL	① ② ③ ④ ⑤ ⑥ ⑦ ⑧ ⑨ ⑩
TOUCHING THINGS REPEATEDLY	① ② ③ ④ ⑤ ⑥ ⑦ ⑧ ⑨ ⑩
DIFFICULT SLEEPING	① ② ③ ④ ⑤ ⑥ ⑦ ⑧ ⑨ ⑩

IMPULSIVITY

ACTING WITHOUT THINKING	① ② ③ ④ ⑤ ⑥ ⑦ ⑧ ⑨ ⑩
INTERRUPTING OTHERS	① ② ③ ④ ⑤ ⑥ ⑦ ⑧ ⑨ ⑩
EASILY FRUSTRATED	① ② ③ ④ ⑤ ⑥ ⑦ ⑧ ⑨ ⑩
UNABLE TO HOLD BACKE MOTIONS	① ② ③ ④ ⑤ ⑥ ⑦ ⑧ ⑨ ⑩

MEALS

MEDICATIONS

WATER TRACKER

NOTES

....
....

DAY GOALS

1 ....
2 ....
3 ....

DATE

WEEK

LOCATION

WEIGHT

MOOD TRACKER

BEHAVIOR

INATTENTION

SHORT ATTENTION	① ② ③ ④ ⑤ ⑥ ⑦ ⑧ ⑨ ⑩
UNMOTIVATED / BORED	① ② ③ ④ ⑤ ⑥ ⑦ ⑧ ⑨ ⑩
SHORT ATTENTION	① ② ③ ④ ⑤ ⑥ ⑦ ⑧ ⑨ ⑩
FORGETFUL / CONFUSIONED	① ② ③ ④ ⑤ ⑥ ⑦ ⑧ ⑨ ⑩

HYPERACTIVITY

CONSTANTLY MOVING / TALKING	① ② ③ ④ ⑤ ⑥ ⑦ ⑧ ⑨ ⑩
STRUGGLING TO SIT STILL	① ② ③ ④ ⑤ ⑥ ⑦ ⑧ ⑨ ⑩
TOUCHING THINGS REPEATEDLY	① ② ③ ④ ⑤ ⑥ ⑦ ⑧ ⑨ ⑩
DIFFICULT SLEEPING	① ② ③ ④ ⑤ ⑥ ⑦ ⑧ ⑨ ⑩

IMPULSIVITY

ACTING WITHOUT THINKING	① ② ③ ④ ⑤ ⑥ ⑦ ⑧ ⑨ ⑩
INTERRUPTING OTHERS	① ② ③ ④ ⑤ ⑥ ⑦ ⑧ ⑨ ⑩
EASILY FRUSTRATED	① ② ③ ④ ⑤ ⑥ ⑦ ⑧ ⑨ ⑩
UNABLE TO HOLD BACKE MOTIONS	① ② ③ ④ ⑤ ⑥ ⑦ ⑧ ⑨ ⑩

MEALS

MEDICATIONS

WATER TRACKER

NOTES

....
....

DAY GOALS

1 ....
2 ....
3 ....

DATE
WEEK
LOCATION
WEIGHT

MOOD TRACKER

BEHAVIOR

INATTENTION

SHORT ATTENTION	① ② ③ ④ ⑤ ⑥ ⑦ ⑧ ⑨ ⑩
UNMOTIVATED / BORED	① ② ③ ④ ⑤ ⑥ ⑦ ⑧ ⑨ ⑩
SHORT ATTENTION	① ② ③ ④ ⑤ ⑥ ⑦ ⑧ ⑨ ⑩
FORGETFUL / CONFUSIONED	① ② ③ ④ ⑤ ⑥ ⑦ ⑧ ⑨ ⑩

HYPERACTIVITY

CONSTANTLY MOVING / TALKING	① ② ③ ④ ⑤ ⑥ ⑦ ⑧ ⑨ ⑩
STRUGGLING TO SIT STILL	① ② ③ ④ ⑤ ⑥ ⑦ ⑧ ⑨ ⑩
TOUCHING THINGS REPEATEDLY	① ② ③ ④ ⑤ ⑥ ⑦ ⑧ ⑨ ⑩
DIFFICULT SLEEPING	① ② ③ ④ ⑤ ⑥ ⑦ ⑧ ⑨ ⑩

IMPULSIVITY

ACTING WITHOUT THINKING	① ② ③ ④ ⑤ ⑥ ⑦ ⑧ ⑨ ⑩
INTERRUPTING OTHERS	① ② ③ ④ ⑤ ⑥ ⑦ ⑧ ⑨ ⑩
EASILY FRUSTRATED	① ② ③ ④ ⑤ ⑥ ⑦ ⑧ ⑨ ⑩
UNABLE TO HOLD BACKE MOTIONS	① ② ③ ④ ⑤ ⑥ ⑦ ⑧ ⑨ ⑩

MEALS

MEDICATIONS

WATER TRACKER

NOTES

....
....

DAY GOALS

1 ....
2 ....
3 ....

DATE
WEEK
LOCATION
WEIGHT

MOOD TRACKER

😞 😐 😖 😢 😠 😄

BEHAVIOR

INATTENTION

SHORT ATTENTION	① ② ③ ④ ⑤ ⑥ ⑦ ⑧ ⑨ ⑩
UNMOTIVATED / BORED	① ② ③ ④ ⑤ ⑥ ⑦ ⑧ ⑨ ⑩
SHORT ATTENTION	① ② ③ ④ ⑤ ⑥ ⑦ ⑧ ⑨ ⑩
FORGETFUL / CONFUSIONED	① ② ③ ④ ⑤ ⑥ ⑦ ⑧ ⑨ ⑩

HYPERACTIVITY

CONSTANTLY MOVING / TALKING	① ② ③ ④ ⑤ ⑥ ⑦ ⑧ ⑨ ⑩
STRUGGLING TO SIT STILL	① ② ③ ④ ⑤ ⑥ ⑦ ⑧ ⑨ ⑩
TOUCHING THINGS REPEATEDLY	① ② ③ ④ ⑤ ⑥ ⑦ ⑧ ⑨ ⑩
DIFFICULT SLEEPING	① ② ③ ④ ⑤ ⑥ ⑦ ⑧ ⑨ ⑩

IMPULSIVITY

ACTING WITHOUT THINKING	① ② ③ ④ ⑤ ⑥ ⑦ ⑧ ⑨ ⑩
INTERRUPTING OTHERS	① ② ③ ④ ⑤ ⑥ ⑦ ⑧ ⑨ ⑩
EASILY FRUSTRATED	① ② ③ ④ ⑤ ⑥ ⑦ ⑧ ⑨ ⑩
UNABLE TO HOLD BACKE MOTIONS	① ② ③ ④ ⑤ ⑥ ⑦ ⑧ ⑨ ⑩

MEALS

MEDICATIONS

WATER TRACKER

▯ ▯ ▯ ▯ ▯ ▯ ▯

NOTES

....
....

DAY GOALS

1 ....
2 ....
3 ....

DATE

WEEK

LOCATION

WEIGHT

MOOD TRACKER

$\odot$ $\odot$ $\odot$ $\odot$ $\odot$ $\odot$

BEHAVIOR

INATTENTION

SHORT ATTENTION	① ② ③ ④ ⑤ ⑥ ⑦ ⑧ ⑨ ⑩
UNMOTIVATED / BORED	① ② ③ ④ ⑤ ⑥ ⑦ ⑧ ⑨ ⑩
SHORT ATTENTION	① ② ③ ④ ⑤ ⑥ ⑦ ⑧ ⑨ ⑩
FORGETFUL / CONFUSIONED	① ② ③ ④ ⑤ ⑥ ⑦ ⑧ ⑨ ⑩

HYPERACTIVITY

CONSTANTLY MOVING / TALKING	① ② ③ ④ ⑤ ⑥ ⑦ ⑧ ⑨ ⑩
STRUGGLING TO SIT STILL	① ② ③ ④ ⑤ ⑥ ⑦ ⑧ ⑨ ⑩
TOUCHING THINGS REPEATEDLY	① ② ③ ④ ⑤ ⑥ ⑦ ⑧ ⑨ ⑩
DIFFICULT SLEEPING	① ② ③ ④ ⑤ ⑥ ⑦ ⑧ ⑨ ⑩

IMPULSIVITY

ACTING WITHOUT THINKING	① ② ③ ④ ⑤ ⑥ ⑦ ⑧ ⑨ ⑩
INTERRUPTING OTHERS	① ② ③ ④ ⑤ ⑥ ⑦ ⑧ ⑨ ⑩
EASILY FRUSTRATED	① ② ③ ④ ⑤ ⑥ ⑦ ⑧ ⑨ ⑩
UNABLE TO HOLD BACKE MOTIONS	① ② ③ ④ ⑤ ⑥ ⑦ ⑧ ⑨ ⑩

MEALS

MEDICATIONS

WATER TRACKER

NOTES

....
....

DAY GOALS

1 ....
2 ....
3 ....

DATE

WEEK

LOCATION

WEIGHT

MOOD TRACKER

BEHAVIOR

INATTENTION

SHORT ATTENTION	① ② ③ ④ ⑤ ⑥ ⑦ ⑧ ⑨ ⑩
UNMOTIVATED / BORED	① ② ③ ④ ⑤ ⑥ ⑦ ⑧ ⑨ ⑩
SHORT ATTENTION	① ② ③ ④ ⑤ ⑥ ⑦ ⑧ ⑨ ⑩
FORGETFUL / CONFUSIONED	① ② ③ ④ ⑤ ⑥ ⑦ ⑧ ⑨ ⑩

HYPERACTIVITY

CONSTANTLY MOVING / TALKING	① ② ③ ④ ⑤ ⑥ ⑦ ⑧ ⑨ ⑩
STRUGGLING TO SIT STILL	① ② ③ ④ ⑤ ⑥ ⑦ ⑧ ⑨ ⑩
TOUCHING THINGS REPEATEDLY	① ② ③ ④ ⑤ ⑥ ⑦ ⑧ ⑨ ⑩
DIFFICULT SLEEPING	① ② ③ ④ ⑤ ⑥ ⑦ ⑧ ⑨ ⑩

IMPULSIVITY

ACTING WITHOUT THINKING	① ② ③ ④ ⑤ ⑥ ⑦ ⑧ ⑨ ⑩
INTERRUPTING OTHERS	① ② ③ ④ ⑤ ⑥ ⑦ ⑧ ⑨ ⑩
EASILY FRUSTRATED	① ② ③ ④ ⑤ ⑥ ⑦ ⑧ ⑨ ⑩
UNABLE TO HOLD BACKE MOTIONS	① ② ③ ④ ⑤ ⑥ ⑦ ⑧ ⑨ ⑩

MEALS

MEDICATIONS

WATER TRACKER

NOTES

....
....

DAY GOALS

1 ....
2 ....
3 ....

DATE

WEEK

LOCATION

WEIGHT

MOOD TRACKER

BEHAVIOR

INATTENTION

SHORT ATTENTION	① ② ③ ④ ⑤ ⑥ ⑦ ⑧ ⑨ ⑩
UNMOTIVATED / BORED	① ② ③ ④ ⑤ ⑥ ⑦ ⑧ ⑨ ⑩
SHORT ATTENTION	① ② ③ ④ ⑤ ⑥ ⑦ ⑧ ⑨ ⑩
FORGETFUL / CONFUSIONED	① ② ③ ④ ⑤ ⑥ ⑦ ⑧ ⑨ ⑩

HYPERACTIVITY

CONSTANTLY MOVING / TALKING	① ② ③ ④ ⑤ ⑥ ⑦ ⑧ ⑨ ⑩
STRUGGLING TO SIT STILL	① ② ③ ④ ⑤ ⑥ ⑦ ⑧ ⑨ ⑩
TOUCHING THINGS REPEATEDLY	① ② ③ ④ ⑤ ⑥ ⑦ ⑧ ⑨ ⑩
DIFFICULT SLEEPING	① ② ③ ④ ⑤ ⑥ ⑦ ⑧ ⑨ ⑩

IMPULSIVITY

ACTING WITHOUT THINKING	① ② ③ ④ ⑤ ⑥ ⑦ ⑧ ⑨ ⑩
INTERRUPTING OTHERS	① ② ③ ④ ⑤ ⑥ ⑦ ⑧ ⑨ ⑩
EASILY FRUSTRATED	① ② ③ ④ ⑤ ⑥ ⑦ ⑧ ⑨ ⑩
UNABLE TO HOLD BACKE MOTIONS	① ② ③ ④ ⑤ ⑥ ⑦ ⑧ ⑨ ⑩

MEALS

MEDICATIONS

WATER TRACKER

NOTES

....
....

DAY GOALS

1 ....
2 ....
3 ....

DATE

WEEK

LOCATION

WEIGHT

MOOD TRACKER

$\odot$ $\odot$ $\odot$ $\odot$ $\odot$ $\odot$

BEHAVIOR

INATTENTION

SHORT ATTENTION	① ② ③ ④ ⑤ ⑥ ⑦ ⑧ ⑨ ⑩
UNMOTIVATED / BORED	① ② ③ ④ ⑤ ⑥ ⑦ ⑧ ⑨ ⑩
SHORT ATTENTION	① ② ③ ④ ⑤ ⑥ ⑦ ⑧ ⑨ ⑩
FORGETFUL / CONFUSIONED	① ② ③ ④ ⑤ ⑥ ⑦ ⑧ ⑨ ⑩

HYPERACTIVITY

CONSTANTLY MOVING / TALKING	① ② ③ ④ ⑤ ⑥ ⑦ ⑧ ⑨ ⑩
STRUGGLING TO SIT STILL	① ② ③ ④ ⑤ ⑥ ⑦ ⑧ ⑨ ⑩
TOUCHING THINGS REPEATEDLY	① ② ③ ④ ⑤ ⑥ ⑦ ⑧ ⑨ ⑩
DIFFICULT SLEEPING	① ② ③ ④ ⑤ ⑥ ⑦ ⑧ ⑨ ⑩

IMPULSIVITY

ACTING WITHOUT THINKING	① ② ③ ④ ⑤ ⑥ ⑦ ⑧ ⑨ ⑩
INTERRUPTING OTHERS	① ② ③ ④ ⑤ ⑥ ⑦ ⑧ ⑨ ⑩
EASILY FRUSTRATED	① ② ③ ④ ⑤ ⑥ ⑦ ⑧ ⑨ ⑩
UNABLE TO HOLD BACKE MOTIONS	① ② ③ ④ ⑤ ⑥ ⑦ ⑧ ⑨ ⑩

MEALS

MEDICATIONS

WATER TRACKER

NOTES

....
....

DAY GOALS

1 ....
2 ....
3 ....

DATE

WEEK

LOCATION

WEIGHT

MOOD TRACKER

BEHAVIOR

INATTENTION

SHORT ATTENTION	① ② ③ ④ ⑤ ⑥ ⑦ ⑧ ⑨ ⑩
UNMOTIVATED / BORED	① ② ③ ④ ⑤ ⑥ ⑦ ⑧ ⑨ ⑩
SHORT ATTENTION	① ② ③ ④ ⑤ ⑥ ⑦ ⑧ ⑨ ⑩
FORGETFUL / CONFUSIONED	① ② ③ ④ ⑤ ⑥ ⑦ ⑧ ⑨ ⑩

HYPERACTIVITY

CONSTANTLY MOVING / TALKING	① ② ③ ④ ⑤ ⑥ ⑦ ⑧ ⑨ ⑩
STRUGGLING TO SIT STILL	① ② ③ ④ ⑤ ⑥ ⑦ ⑧ ⑨ ⑩
TOUCHING THINGS REPEATEDLY	① ② ③ ④ ⑤ ⑥ ⑦ ⑧ ⑨ ⑩
DIFFICULT SLEEPING	① ② ③ ④ ⑤ ⑥ ⑦ ⑧ ⑨ ⑩

IMPULSIVITY

ACTING WITHOUT THINKING	① ② ③ ④ ⑤ ⑥ ⑦ ⑧ ⑨ ⑩
INTERRUPTING OTHERS	① ② ③ ④ ⑤ ⑥ ⑦ ⑧ ⑨ ⑩
EASILY FRUSTRATED	① ② ③ ④ ⑤ ⑥ ⑦ ⑧ ⑨ ⑩
UNABLE TO HOLD BACKE MOTIONS	① ② ③ ④ ⑤ ⑥ ⑦ ⑧ ⑨ ⑩

MEALS

MEDICATIONS

WATER TRACKER

NOTES

....
....

DAY GOALS

1 ....
2 ....
3 ....

DATE

WEEK

LOCATION

WEIGHT

MOOD TRACKER

BEHAVIOR

INATTENTION

SHORT ATTENTION	① ② ③ ④ ⑤ ⑥ ⑦ ⑧ ⑨ ⑩
UNMOTIVATED / BORED	① ② ③ ④ ⑤ ⑥ ⑦ ⑧ ⑨ ⑩
SHORT ATTENTION	① ② ③ ④ ⑤ ⑥ ⑦ ⑧ ⑨ ⑩
FORGETFUL / CONFUSIONED	① ② ③ ④ ⑤ ⑥ ⑦ ⑧ ⑨ ⑩

HYPERACTIVITY

CONSTANTLY MOVING / TALKING	① ② ③ ④ ⑤ ⑥ ⑦ ⑧ ⑨ ⑩
STRUGGLING TO SIT STILL	① ② ③ ④ ⑤ ⑥ ⑦ ⑧ ⑨ ⑩
TOUCHING THINGS REPEATEDLY	① ② ③ ④ ⑤ ⑥ ⑦ ⑧ ⑨ ⑩
DIFFICULT SLEEPING	① ② ③ ④ ⑤ ⑥ ⑦ ⑧ ⑨ ⑩

IMPULSIVITY

ACTING WITHOUT THINKING	① ② ③ ④ ⑤ ⑥ ⑦ ⑧ ⑨ ⑩
INTERRUPTING OTHERS	① ② ③ ④ ⑤ ⑥ ⑦ ⑧ ⑨ ⑩
EASILY FRUSTRATED	① ② ③ ④ ⑤ ⑥ ⑦ ⑧ ⑨ ⑩
UNABLE TO HOLD BACKE MOTIONS	① ② ③ ④ ⑤ ⑥ ⑦ ⑧ ⑨ ⑩

MEALS

MEDICATIONS

WATER TRACKER

NOTES

....
....

1 ....
2 ....
3 ....

DATE
WEEK
LOCATION
WEIGHT

MOOD TRACKER

BEHAVIOR

INATTENTION

SHORT ATTENTION	(1)(2)(3)(4)(5)(6)(7)(8)(9)(10)
UNMOTIVATED / BORED	(1)(2)(3)(4)(5)(6)(7)(8)(9)(10)
SHORT ATTENTION	(1)(2)(3)(4)(5)(6)(7)(8)(9)(10)
FORGETFUL / CONFUSIONED	(1)(2)(3)(4)(5)(6)(7)(8)(9)(10)

HYPERACTIVITY

CONSTANTLY MOVING / TALKING	(1)(2)(3)(4)(5)(6)(7)(8)(9)(10)
STRUGGLING TO SIT STILL	(1)(2)(3)(4)(5)(6)(7)(8)(9)(10)
TOUCHING THINGS REPEATEDLY	(1)(2)(3)(4)(5)(6)(7)(8)(9)(10)
DIFFICULT SLEEPING	(1)(2)(3)(4)(5)(6)(7)(8)(9)(10)

IMPULSIVITY

ACTING WITHOUT THINKING	(1)(2)(3)(4)(5)(6)(7)(8)(9)(10)
INTERRUPTING OTHERS	(1)(2)(3)(4)(5)(6)(7)(8)(9)(10)
EASILY FRUSTRATED	(1)(2)(3)(4)(5)(6)(7)(8)(9)(10)
UNABLE TO HOLD BACKE MOTIONS	(1)(2)(3)(4)(5)(6)(7)(8)(9)(10)

MEALS

MEDICATIONS

WATER TRACKER

NOTES

....
....

DAY GOALS

1 ....
2 ....
3 ....

DATE
WEEK
LOCATION
WEIGHT

MOOD TRACKER

BEHAVIOR

INATTENTION

SHORT ATTENTION	① ② ③ ④ ⑤ ⑥ ⑦ ⑧ ⑨ ⑩
UNMOTIVATED / BORED	① ② ③ ④ ⑤ ⑥ ⑦ ⑧ ⑨ ⑩
SHORT ATTENTION	① ② ③ ④ ⑤ ⑥ ⑦ ⑧ ⑨ ⑩
FORGETFUL / CONFUSIONED	① ② ③ ④ ⑤ ⑥ ⑦ ⑧ ⑨ ⑩

HYPERACTIVITY

CONSTANTLY MOVING / TALKING	① ② ③ ④ ⑤ ⑥ ⑦ ⑧ ⑨ ⑩
STRUGGLING TO SIT STILL	① ② ③ ④ ⑤ ⑥ ⑦ ⑧ ⑨ ⑩
TOUCHING THINGS REPEATEDLY	① ② ③ ④ ⑤ ⑥ ⑦ ⑧ ⑨ ⑩
DIFFICULT SLEEPING	① ② ③ ④ ⑤ ⑥ ⑦ ⑧ ⑨ ⑩

IMPULSIVITY

ACTING WITHOUT THINKING	① ② ③ ④ ⑤ ⑥ ⑦ ⑧ ⑨ ⑩
INTERRUPTING OTHERS	① ② ③ ④ ⑤ ⑥ ⑦ ⑧ ⑨ ⑩
EASILY FRUSTRATED	① ② ③ ④ ⑤ ⑥ ⑦ ⑧ ⑨ ⑩
UNABLE TO HOLD BACKE MOTIONS	① ② ③ ④ ⑤ ⑥ ⑦ ⑧ ⑨ ⑩

MEALS

MEDICATIONS

WATER TRACKER

NOTES

....
....

DAY GOALS

1 ....
2 ....
3 ....

DATE
WEEK
LOCATION
WEIGHT

MOOD TRACKER

BEHAVIOR

INATTENTION

SHORT ATTENTION	① ② ③ ④ ⑤ ⑥ ⑦ ⑧ ⑨ ⑩
UNMOTIVATED / BORED	① ② ③ ④ ⑤ ⑥ ⑦ ⑧ ⑨ ⑩
SHORT ATTENTION	① ② ③ ④ ⑤ ⑥ ⑦ ⑧ ⑨ ⑩
FORGETFUL / CONFUSIONED	① ② ③ ④ ⑤ ⑥ ⑦ ⑧ ⑨ ⑩

HYPERACTIVITY

CONSTANTLY MOVING / TALKING	① ② ③ ④ ⑤ ⑥ ⑦ ⑧ ⑨ ⑩
STRUGGLING TO SIT STILL	① ② ③ ④ ⑤ ⑥ ⑦ ⑧ ⑨ ⑩
TOUCHING THINGS REPEATEDLY	① ② ③ ④ ⑤ ⑥ ⑦ ⑧ ⑨ ⑩
DIFFICULT SLEEPING	① ② ③ ④ ⑤ ⑥ ⑦ ⑧ ⑨ ⑩

IMPULSIVITY

ACTING WITHOUT THINKING	① ② ③ ④ ⑤ ⑥ ⑦ ⑧ ⑨ ⑩
INTERRUPTING OTHERS	① ② ③ ④ ⑤ ⑥ ⑦ ⑧ ⑨ ⑩
EASILY FRUSTRATED	① ② ③ ④ ⑤ ⑥ ⑦ ⑧ ⑨ ⑩
UNABLE TO HOLD BACKE MOTIONS	① ② ③ ④ ⑤ ⑥ ⑦ ⑧ ⑨ ⑩

MEALS

MEDICATIONS

WATER TRACKER

NOTES

....
....

DAY GOALS

1 ....
2 ....
3 ....

DATE
WEEK
LOCATION
WEIGHT

MOOD TRACKER

BEHAVIOR

INATTENTION

SHORT ATTENTION	① ② ③ ④ ⑤ ⑥ ⑦ ⑧ ⑨ ⑩
UNMOTIVATED / BORED	① ② ③ ④ ⑤ ⑥ ⑦ ⑧ ⑨ ⑩
SHORT ATTENTION	① ② ③ ④ ⑤ ⑥ ⑦ ⑧ ⑨ ⑩
FORGETFUL / CONFUSIONED	① ② ③ ④ ⑤ ⑥ ⑦ ⑧ ⑨ ⑩

HYPERACTIVITY

CONSTANTLY MOVING / TALKING	① ② ③ ④ ⑤ ⑥ ⑦ ⑧ ⑨ ⑩
STRUGGLING TO SIT STILL	① ② ③ ④ ⑤ ⑥ ⑦ ⑧ ⑨ ⑩
TOUCHING THINGS REPEATEDLY	① ② ③ ④ ⑤ ⑥ ⑦ ⑧ ⑨ ⑩
DIFFICULT SLEEPING	① ② ③ ④ ⑤ ⑥ ⑦ ⑧ ⑨ ⑩

IMPULSIVITY

ACTING WITHOUT THINKING	① ② ③ ④ ⑤ ⑥ ⑦ ⑧ ⑨ ⑩
INTERRUPTING OTHERS	① ② ③ ④ ⑤ ⑥ ⑦ ⑧ ⑨ ⑩
EASILY FRUSTRATED	① ② ③ ④ ⑤ ⑥ ⑦ ⑧ ⑨ ⑩
UNABLE TO HOLD BACKE MOTIONS	① ② ③ ④ ⑤ ⑥ ⑦ ⑧ ⑨ ⑩

MEALS

MEDICATIONS

WATER TRACKER

NOTES

....
....

DAY GOALS

1 ....
2 ....
3 ....

DATE
WEEK
LOCATION
WEIGHT

MOOD TRACKER

BEHAVIOR

INATTENTION

SHORT ATTENTION	① ② ③ ④ ⑤ ⑥ ⑦ ⑧ ⑨ ⑩
UNMOTIVATED / BORED	① ② ③ ④ ⑤ ⑥ ⑦ ⑧ ⑨ ⑩
SHORT ATTENTION	① ② ③ ④ ⑤ ⑥ ⑦ ⑧ ⑨ ⑩
FORGETFUL / CONFUSIONED	① ② ③ ④ ⑤ ⑥ ⑦ ⑧ ⑨ ⑩

HYPERACTIVITY

CONSTANTLY MOVING / TALKING	① ② ③ ④ ⑤ ⑥ ⑦ ⑧ ⑨ ⑩
STRUGGLING TO SIT STILL	① ② ③ ④ ⑤ ⑥ ⑦ ⑧ ⑨ ⑩
TOUCHING THINGS REPEATEDLY	① ② ③ ④ ⑤ ⑥ ⑦ ⑧ ⑨ ⑩
DIFFICULT SLEEPING	① ② ③ ④ ⑤ ⑥ ⑦ ⑧ ⑨ ⑩

IMPULSIVITY

ACTING WITHOUT THINKING	① ② ③ ④ ⑤ ⑥ ⑦ ⑧ ⑨ ⑩
INTERRUPTING OTHERS	① ② ③ ④ ⑤ ⑥ ⑦ ⑧ ⑨ ⑩
EASILY FRUSTRATED	① ② ③ ④ ⑤ ⑥ ⑦ ⑧ ⑨ ⑩
UNABLE TO HOLD BACKE MOTIONS	① ② ③ ④ ⑤ ⑥ ⑦ ⑧ ⑨ ⑩

MEALS

MEDICATIONS

WATER TRACKER

NOTES

....
....

DAY GOALS

1 ....
2 ....
3 ....

DATE

WEEK

LOCATION

WEIGHT

MOOD TRACKER

BEHAVIOR

INATTENTION

SHORT ATTENTION	① ② ③ ④ ⑤ ⑥ ⑦ ⑧ ⑨ ⑩
UNMOTIVATED / BORED	① ② ③ ④ ⑤ ⑥ ⑦ ⑧ ⑨ ⑩
SHORT ATTENTION	① ② ③ ④ ⑤ ⑥ ⑦ ⑧ ⑨ ⑩
FORGETFUL / CONFUSIONED	① ② ③ ④ ⑤ ⑥ ⑦ ⑧ ⑨ ⑩

HYPERACTIVITY

CONSTANTLY MOVING / TALKING	① ② ③ ④ ⑤ ⑥ ⑦ ⑧ ⑨ ⑩
STRUGGLING TO SIT STILL	① ② ③ ④ ⑤ ⑥ ⑦ ⑧ ⑨ ⑩
TOUCHING THINGS REPEATEDLY	① ② ③ ④ ⑤ ⑥ ⑦ ⑧ ⑨ ⑩
DIFFICULT SLEEPING	① ② ③ ④ ⑤ ⑥ ⑦ ⑧ ⑨ ⑩

IMPULSIVITY

ACTING WITHOUT THINKING	① ② ③ ④ ⑤ ⑥ ⑦ ⑧ ⑨ ⑩
INTERRUPTING OTHERS	① ② ③ ④ ⑤ ⑥ ⑦ ⑧ ⑨ ⑩
EASILY FRUSTRATED	① ② ③ ④ ⑤ ⑥ ⑦ ⑧ ⑨ ⑩
UNABLE TO HOLD BACKE MOTIONS	① ② ③ ④ ⑤ ⑥ ⑦ ⑧ ⑨ ⑩

MEALS

MEDICATIONS

WATER TRACKER

NOTES

....
....

DAY GOALS

1 ....
2 ....
3 ....

DATE
WEEK
LOCATION
WEIGHT

MOOD TRACKER

BEHAVIOR

INATTENTION

SHORT ATTENTION	① ② ③ ④ ⑤ ⑥ ⑦ ⑧ ⑨ ⑩
UNMOTIVATED / BORED	① ② ③ ④ ⑤ ⑥ ⑦ ⑧ ⑨ ⑩
SHORT ATTENTION	① ② ③ ④ ⑤ ⑥ ⑦ ⑧ ⑨ ⑩
FORGETFUL / CONFUSIONED	① ② ③ ④ ⑤ ⑥ ⑦ ⑧ ⑨ ⑩

HYPERACTIVITY

CONSTANTLY MOVING / TALKING	① ② ③ ④ ⑤ ⑥ ⑦ ⑧ ⑨ ⑩
STRUGGLING TO SIT STILL	① ② ③ ④ ⑤ ⑥ ⑦ ⑧ ⑨ ⑩
TOUCHING THINGS REPEATEDLY	① ② ③ ④ ⑤ ⑥ ⑦ ⑧ ⑨ ⑩
DIFFICULT SLEEPING	① ② ③ ④ ⑤ ⑥ ⑦ ⑧ ⑨ ⑩

IMPULSIVITY

ACTING WITHOUT THINKING	① ② ③ ④ ⑤ ⑥ ⑦ ⑧ ⑨ ⑩
INTERRUPTING OTHERS	① ② ③ ④ ⑤ ⑥ ⑦ ⑧ ⑨ ⑩
EASILY FRUSTRATED	① ② ③ ④ ⑤ ⑥ ⑦ ⑧ ⑨ ⑩
UNABLE TO HOLD BACKE MOTIONS	① ② ③ ④ ⑤ ⑥ ⑦ ⑧ ⑨ ⑩

MEALS

MEDICATIONS

WATER TRACKER

NOTES

....
....

1 ....

2 ....

3 ....

DATE

WEEK

LOCATION

WEIGHT

MOOD TRACKER

BEHAVIOR

INATTENTION

SHORT ATTENTION	1 2 3 4 5 6 7 8 9 10
UNMOTIVATED / BORED	1 2 3 4 5 6 7 8 9 10
SHORT ATTENTION	1 2 3 4 5 6 7 8 9 10
FORGETFUL / CONFUSIONED	1 2 3 4 5 6 7 8 9 10

HYPERACTIVITY

CONSTANTLY MOVING / TALKING	1 2 3 4 5 6 7 8 9 10
STRUGGLING TO SIT STILL	1 2 3 4 5 6 7 8 9 10
TOUCHING THINGS REPEATEDLY	1 2 3 4 5 6 7 8 9 10
DIFFICULT SLEEPING	1 2 3 4 5 6 7 8 9 10

IMPULSIVITY

ACTING WITHOUT THINKING	1 2 3 4 5 6 7 8 9 10
INTERRUPTING OTHERS	1 2 3 4 5 6 7 8 9 10
EASILY FRUSTRATED	1 2 3 4 5 6 7 8 9 10
UNABLE TO HOLD BACKE MOTIONS	1 2 3 4 5 6 7 8 9 10

MEALS

MEDICATIONS

WATER TRACKER

NOTES

....

....

DAY GOALS

1 ....
2 ....
3 ....

DATE
WEEK
LOCATION
WEIGHT

MOOD TRACKER

BEHAVIOR

INATTENTION

SHORT ATTENTION	① ② ③ ④ ⑤ ⑥ ⑦ ⑧ ⑨ ⑩
UNMOTIVATED / BORED	① ② ③ ④ ⑤ ⑥ ⑦ ⑧ ⑨ ⑩
SHORT ATTENTION	① ② ③ ④ ⑤ ⑥ ⑦ ⑧ ⑨ ⑩
FORGETFUL / CONFUSIONED	① ② ③ ④ ⑤ ⑥ ⑦ ⑧ ⑨ ⑩

HYPERACTIVITY

CONSTANTLY MOVING / TALKING	① ② ③ ④ ⑤ ⑥ ⑦ ⑧ ⑨ ⑩
STRUGGLING TO SIT STILL	① ② ③ ④ ⑤ ⑥ ⑦ ⑧ ⑨ ⑩
TOUCHING THINGS REPEATEDLY	① ② ③ ④ ⑤ ⑥ ⑦ ⑧ ⑨ ⑩
DIFFICULT SLEEPING	① ② ③ ④ ⑤ ⑥ ⑦ ⑧ ⑨ ⑩

IMPULSIVITY

ACTING WITHOUT THINKING	① ② ③ ④ ⑤ ⑥ ⑦ ⑧ ⑨ ⑩
INTERRUPTING OTHERS	① ② ③ ④ ⑤ ⑥ ⑦ ⑧ ⑨ ⑩
EASILY FRUSTRATED	① ② ③ ④ ⑤ ⑥ ⑦ ⑧ ⑨ ⑩
UNABLE TO HOLD BACKE MOTIONS	① ② ③ ④ ⑤ ⑥ ⑦ ⑧ ⑨ ⑩

MEALS

MEDICATIONS

WATER TRACKER

NOTES

....
....

1 ....
2 ....
3 ....

DATE

WEEK

LOCATION

WEIGHT

MOOD TRACKER

BEHAVIOR

INATTENTION

SHORT ATTENTION	① ② ③ ④ ⑤ ⑥ ⑦ ⑧ ⑨ ⑩
UNMOTIVATED / BORED	① ② ③ ④ ⑤ ⑥ ⑦ ⑧ ⑨ ⑩
SHORT ATTENTION	① ② ③ ④ ⑤ ⑥ ⑦ ⑧ ⑨ ⑩
FORGETFUL / CONFUSIONED	① ② ③ ④ ⑤ ⑥ ⑦ ⑧ ⑨ ⑩

HYPERACTIVITY

CONSTANTLY MOVING / TALKING	① ② ③ ④ ⑤ ⑥ ⑦ ⑧ ⑨ ⑩
STRUGGLING TO SIT STILL	① ② ③ ④ ⑤ ⑥ ⑦ ⑧ ⑨ ⑩
TOUCHING THINGS REPEATEDLY	① ② ③ ④ ⑤ ⑥ ⑦ ⑧ ⑨ ⑩
DIFFICULT SLEEPING	① ② ③ ④ ⑤ ⑥ ⑦ ⑧ ⑨ ⑩

IMPULSIVITY

ACTING WITHOUT THINKING	① ② ③ ④ ⑤ ⑥ ⑦ ⑧ ⑨ ⑩
INTERRUPTING OTHERS	① ② ③ ④ ⑤ ⑥ ⑦ ⑧ ⑨ ⑩
EASILY FRUSTRATED	① ② ③ ④ ⑤ ⑥ ⑦ ⑧ ⑨ ⑩
UNABLE TO HOLD BACKE MOTIONS	① ② ③ ④ ⑤ ⑥ ⑦ ⑧ ⑨ ⑩

MEALS

MEDICATIONS

WATER TRACKER

NOTES

....
....

DAY GOALS

1 ....
2 ....
3 ....

DATE

WEEK

LOCATION

WEIGHT

MOOD TRACKER

BEHAVIOR

INATTENTION

SHORT ATTENTION	(1)(2)(3)(4)(5)(6)(7)(8)(9)(10)
UNMOTIVATED / BORED	(1)(2)(3)(4)(5)(6)(7)(8)(9)(10)
SHORT ATTENTION	(1)(2)(3)(4)(5)(6)(7)(8)(9)(10)
FORGETFUL / CONFUSIONED	(1)(2)(3)(4)(5)(6)(7)(8)(9)(10)

HYPERACTIVITY

CONSTANTLY MOVING / TALKING	(1)(2)(3)(4)(5)(6)(7)(8)(9)(10)
STRUGGLING TO SIT STILL	(1)(2)(3)(4)(5)(6)(7)(8)(9)(10)
TOUCHING THINGS REPEATEDLY	(1)(2)(3)(4)(5)(6)(7)(8)(9)(10)
DIFFICULT SLEEPING	(1)(2)(3)(4)(5)(6)(7)(8)(9)(10)

IMPULSIVITY

ACTING WITHOUT THINKING	(1)(2)(3)(4)(5)(6)(7)(8)(9)(10)
INTERRUPTING OTHERS	(1)(2)(3)(4)(5)(6)(7)(8)(9)(10)
EASILY FRUSTRATED	(1)(2)(3)(4)(5)(6)(7)(8)(9)(10)
UNABLE TO HOLD BACKE MOTIONS	(1)(2)(3)(4)(5)(6)(7)(8)(9)(10)

MEALS

MEDICATIONS

WATER TRACKER

NOTES

....
....

DAY GOALS

1 ....
2 ....
3 ....

DATE

WEEK

LOCATION

WEIGHT

MOOD TRACKER

BEHAVIOR

INATTENTION

SHORT ATTENTION	① ② ③ ④ ⑤ ⑥ ⑦ ⑧ ⑨ ⑩
UNMOTIVATED / BORED	① ② ③ ④ ⑤ ⑥ ⑦ ⑧ ⑨ ⑩
SHORT ATTENTION	① ② ③ ④ ⑤ ⑥ ⑦ ⑧ ⑨ ⑩
FORGETFUL / CONFUSIONED	① ② ③ ④ ⑤ ⑥ ⑦ ⑧ ⑨ ⑩

HYPERACTIVITY

CONSTANTLY MOVING / TALKING	① ② ③ ④ ⑤ ⑥ ⑦ ⑧ ⑨ ⑩
STRUGGLING TO SIT STILL	① ② ③ ④ ⑤ ⑥ ⑦ ⑧ ⑨ ⑩
TOUCHING THINGS REPEATEDLY	① ② ③ ④ ⑤ ⑥ ⑦ ⑧ ⑨ ⑩
DIFFICULT SLEEPING	① ② ③ ④ ⑤ ⑥ ⑦ ⑧ ⑨ ⑩

IMPULSIVITY

ACTING WITHOUT THINKING	① ② ③ ④ ⑤ ⑥ ⑦ ⑧ ⑨ ⑩
INTERRUPTING OTHERS	① ② ③ ④ ⑤ ⑥ ⑦ ⑧ ⑨ ⑩
EASILY FRUSTRATED	① ② ③ ④ ⑤ ⑥ ⑦ ⑧ ⑨ ⑩
UNABLE TO HOLD BACKE MOTIONS	① ② ③ ④ ⑤ ⑥ ⑦ ⑧ ⑨ ⑩

MEALS

MEDICATIONS

WATER TRACKER

NOTES

....
....

1 ....
2 ....
3 ....

DATE
WEEK
LOCATION
WEIGHT

MOOD TRACKER

BEHAVIOR

INATTENTION

SHORT ATTENTION	① ② ③ ④ ⑤ ⑥ ⑦ ⑧ ⑨ ⑩
UNMOTIVATED / BORED	① ② ③ ④ ⑤ ⑥ ⑦ ⑧ ⑨ ⑩
SHORT ATTENTION	① ② ③ ④ ⑤ ⑥ ⑦ ⑧ ⑨ ⑩
FORGETFUL / CONFUSIONED	① ② ③ ④ ⑤ ⑥ ⑦ ⑧ ⑨ ⑩

HYPERACTIVITY

CONSTANTLY MOVING / TALKING	① ② ③ ④ ⑤ ⑥ ⑦ ⑧ ⑨ ⑩
STRUGGLING TO SIT STILL	① ② ③ ④ ⑤ ⑥ ⑦ ⑧ ⑨ ⑩
TOUCHING THINGS REPEATEDLY	① ② ③ ④ ⑤ ⑥ ⑦ ⑧ ⑨ ⑩
DIFFICULT SLEEPING	① ② ③ ④ ⑤ ⑥ ⑦ ⑧ ⑨ ⑩

IMPULSIVITY

ACTING WITHOUT THINKING	① ② ③ ④ ⑤ ⑥ ⑦ ⑧ ⑨ ⑩
INTERRUPTING OTHERS	① ② ③ ④ ⑤ ⑥ ⑦ ⑧ ⑨ ⑩
EASILY FRUSTRATED	① ② ③ ④ ⑤ ⑥ ⑦ ⑧ ⑨ ⑩
UNABLE TO HOLD BACKE MOTIONS	① ② ③ ④ ⑤ ⑥ ⑦ ⑧ ⑨ ⑩

MEALS

MEDICATIONS

WATER TRACKER

NOTES

....
....

DAY GOALS	DATE
1	WEEK
2	LOCATION
3	WEIGHT

MOOD TRACKER

:-(:-| >:< :'(>:(:-D

BEHAVIOR

INATTENTION

SHORT ATTENTION	① ② ③ ④ ⑤ ⑥ ⑦ ⑧ ⑨ ⑩
UNMOTIVATED / BORED	① ② ③ ④ ⑤ ⑥ ⑦ ⑧ ⑨ ⑩
SHORT ATTENTION	① ② ③ ④ ⑤ ⑥ ⑦ ⑧ ⑨ ⑩
FORGETFUL / CONFUSIONED	① ② ③ ④ ⑤ ⑥ ⑦ ⑧ ⑨ ⑩

HYPERACTIVITY

CONSTANTLY MOVING / TALKING	① ② ③ ④ ⑤ ⑥ ⑦ ⑧ ⑨ ⑩
STRUGGLING TO SIT STILL	① ② ③ ④ ⑤ ⑥ ⑦ ⑧ ⑨ ⑩
TOUCHING THINGS REPEATEDLY	① ② ③ ④ ⑤ ⑥ ⑦ ⑧ ⑨ ⑩
DIFFICULT SLEEPING	① ② ③ ④ ⑤ ⑥ ⑦ ⑧ ⑨ ⑩

IMPULSIVITY

ACTING WITHOUT THINKING	① ② ③ ④ ⑤ ⑥ ⑦ ⑧ ⑨ ⑩
INTERRUPTING OTHERS	① ② ③ ④ ⑤ ⑥ ⑦ ⑧ ⑨ ⑩
EASILY FRUSTRATED	① ② ③ ④ ⑤ ⑥ ⑦ ⑧ ⑨ ⑩
UNABLE TO HOLD BACKE MOTIONS	① ② ③ ④ ⑤ ⑥ ⑦ ⑧ ⑨ ⑩

MEALS

MEDICATIONS

WATER TRACKER

NOTES

....
....

DAY GOALS

1 ....
2 ....
3 ....

DATE

WEEK

LOCATION

WEIGHT

MOOD TRACKER

BEHAVIOR

INATTENTION

SHORT ATTENTION	① ② ③ ④ ⑤ ⑥ ⑦ ⑧ ⑨ ⑩
UNMOTIVATED / BORED	① ② ③ ④ ⑤ ⑥ ⑦ ⑧ ⑨ ⑩
SHORT ATTENTION	① ② ③ ④ ⑤ ⑥ ⑦ ⑧ ⑨ ⑩
FORGETFUL / CONFUSIONED	① ② ③ ④ ⑤ ⑥ ⑦ ⑧ ⑨ ⑩

HYPERACTIVITY

CONSTANTLY MOVING / TALKING	① ② ③ ④ ⑤ ⑥ ⑦ ⑧ ⑨ ⑩
STRUGGLING TO SIT STILL	① ② ③ ④ ⑤ ⑥ ⑦ ⑧ ⑨ ⑩
TOUCHING THINGS REPEATEDLY	① ② ③ ④ ⑤ ⑥ ⑦ ⑧ ⑨ ⑩
DIFFICULT SLEEPING	① ② ③ ④ ⑤ ⑥ ⑦ ⑧ ⑨ ⑩

IMPULSIVITY

ACTING WITHOUT THINKING	① ② ③ ④ ⑤ ⑥ ⑦ ⑧ ⑨ ⑩
INTERRUPTING OTHERS	① ② ③ ④ ⑤ ⑥ ⑦ ⑧ ⑨ ⑩
EASILY FRUSTRATED	① ② ③ ④ ⑤ ⑥ ⑦ ⑧ ⑨ ⑩
UNABLE TO HOLD BACKE MOTIONS	① ② ③ ④ ⑤ ⑥ ⑦ ⑧ ⑨ ⑩

MEALS

MEDICATIONS

WATER TRACKER

NOTES

....
....

Printed in Great Britain
by Amazon

67888757R00071